GLOBALIZATION

The Key Concepts

ISSN 1747-6550

The series aims to cover the core disciplines and the key cross-disciplinary ideas across the Humanities and Social Sciences. Each book isolates the key concepts to map out the theoretical terrain across a specific subject or idea. Designed specifically for student readers, each book in the series includes boxed case material, summary chapter bullet points, annotated guides to further reading and questions for essays and class discussion

Previously published titles in this series

Film: The Key Concepts
Nitzan Ben-Shaul

Forthcoming in this series

Technoculture: The Key Concepts
Debbie Shaw

Design: The Key Concepts
Mark Westgarth and Eleanor Quince

Fashion: The Key Concepts
Jennifer Craik

Food: The Key Concepts
Warren Belasco

New Media: The Key Concepts
Nicholas Gane

Performance: The Key Concepts
Philip Auslander

Photography: The Key Concepts
David Bate

Queer Theory: The Key Concepts
Noreen Giffney

Race: The Key Concepts
C. Richard King

The Body: The Key Concepts
Lisa Blackman

Visual Culture: The Key Concepts
John Lynch

GLOBALIZATION

The Key Concepts

Thomas Hylland Eriksen

BERG

Oxford • New York

First published in 2007 by
Berg
Editorial offices:
1st Floor, Angel Court, 81 St Clements Street, Oxford, OX4 1AW, UK
175 Fifth Avenue, New York, NY 10010, USA

Berg is the imprint of Oxford International Publishers Ltd.

Library of Congress Cataloguing-in-Publication Data

Eriksen, Thomas Hylland.
    Globalization : the key concepts / Thomas Hylland Eriksen.
        p. cm.
    Includes bibliographical references and index.
    ISBN-13: 978-1-84520-523-2 (cloth)
    ISBN-10: 1-84520-523-5 (cloth)
    ISBN-13: 978-1-84520-524-9 (pbk.)
    ISBN-10: 1-84520-524-3 (pbk.)
 1. Anthropology. 2. Globalization. 3. Globalization—Social aspects. I. Title.

GN27.E69 2007
306—dc22

2007018029

British Library Cataloguing-in-Publication Data

A catalogue record for this book is available from the British Library.

ISBN 978 184520 523 2 (Cloth)
       978 184520 524 9 (Paper)

Typeset by JS Typesetting Ltd, Porthcawl, Mid Glamorgan
Printed in the United Kingdom by Biddles Ltd, King's Lynn

www.bergpublishers.com

CONTENTS

PREFACE

My office desk is large and sturdy, ergonomically adjusted to suit a person of my height and constructed by world-class Swedish engineers from the finest mock hardwood and real steel. Yet, lately it has been groaning audibly. The reason is simple: the desk is burdened not just by the usual pile of half-read books and exam papers; it carries the additional weight of a good-sized library on globalization, sorted roughly into about a dozen wavering stacks. These books, which comprise only a small fraction of the total number of volumes dealing with globalization and transnationalism since around 1990 (as well as a few older ones), form the bulk of the source material used to write this book – one is reminded of the old saying about a scholar being a library's means to create another library – together with countless journal articles, newspaper clippings, downloaded texts and a reasonable collection of personal observations. Even to begin to summarize the contents of each book and every important article would be a hopeless, endless (and rather boring) job. And then there are all the other texts, which I haven't read and probably never will. I am reminded of my countryman Tor Åge Bringsværd's short story about the man who collected the first of September, 1972. Realizing that it would be impossible ever to acquire an overview of everything, he decided to narrow his ambitions, and to become an expert on one single day, namely the first of September. However, the project soon required him to learn new languages, to order tapes of Russian radio broadcasts and late editions of Brazilian newspapers. Of course, although he was at it for years, the poor man went insane long before he was done.

As I began to take notes for this book in February 2006, pondering where to begin to tackle globalization – a topic that is huge in every way – an event in the outside world came to my rescue, as is so often the case with us academics. I had just been reading two very different books about globalization. The American journalist Thomas Friedman, in his ambitious *The World is Flat* (Friedman 2005), described an increasingly integrated world market where 'the playing field had been levelled' in the sense that Indian, Chinese, North Atlantic and other companies were competing with few impediments: his integrated world was a place where capitalism had won and where the fittest would survive, like it or not. Worrying about the future of the

American job market, Friedman noted the emergence of China as a rising power in the global economy, and spoke about the Internet and global financial markets as guarantors for global economic growth.

The other book was James Lovelock's *The Revenge of Gaia* (Lovelock 2006), a deeply pessimistic book about climate change and environmental destruction, where the author argued that the Earth's self-regulating mechanisms were beginning to falter in the face of massive human energy use, with unforeseeable but doubtless enormous consequences. A different take on globalization from Friedman's upbeat assessment of global capitalism, Lovelock's book indicated an important way in which globalization creates universal vulnerability.

Thinking about these books and how to compare them, I glanced at my morning paper to be met by a picture from an animated demonstration in a Middle Eastern city. The reason for this demonstration, and subsequent acts of sabotage, consumer boycott and a brief diplomatic crisis, was the publication, some months earlier, of twelve cartoons depicting the Prophet Mohammed in a leading Danish newspaper. Few of the cartoons could be described as offensive in their content, but there is a general ban against depictions of the Prophet in Sunni Islam, and many Muslims outside (and not least inside) Denmark felt that their dissemination was a deliberate act of humiliation. Regardless of his motivation for commissioning the cartoons, the Danish editor could not have anticipated the reactions, fanning out across the Muslim world and, through its repercussions, damaging relations between Denmark and several Muslim countries.

Thinking about the implications of the cartoon controversy for our attempts to understand globalization, it occurred to me that the affair had demonstrated that not only are political, economic, cultural and ecological issues globalized these days, but so are emotional ones, in this case the feeling of humiliation and offence. One can no longer publish a critique of Islam (or Judaism, or Hinduism etc.) intended for a local readership assured that it will not be read and possibly misunderstood anywhere else. Not all messages travel freely and swiftly in a globalized world, but all have the potential to do so.

We live in a shrunken world: a world of contacts, frictions, comparisons, communication and movement, unrestricted by distance. At the same time, many activities continue to take place without any consequences beyond the local. The aim of this book is to outline some of the main dimensions of globalization and to indicate some ways in which they are being studied and critiqued. Far from being a comprehensive overview of the area, at least this book is an attempt to open more doors than it closes and to point the reader in directions that I have myself found fruitful.

Not many people have been directly involved with this book, but those who have – two anonymous referees and Berg's Tristan Palmer – have given me enough resistance and encouragement to improve substantially on the first draft, and for this I am grateful. Kristin Opsahl Alvarez tracked down and copied a vast number of relevant articles for me – thanks Kristin! Of more enduring, if less direct, significance, is my association with the Transnational Flows group at the University of Oslo (2001–4), directed by Marianne E. Lien (this book fulfils some of my outstanding obligations towards the programme); my more recent collaboration on the anthropology of human security with colleagues at the Free University of Amsterdam (2003–6), under the leadership of Oscar Salemink; and, finally, my participation in various intellectual configurations over the years with Oscar Hemer and Malmö University College. Many others could have been mentioned, but one will have to suffice: it was Eduardo Archetti who put me on the track many years ago and, until his premature death in June 2005, we discussed the topics featured in this book (and many other things) so incessantly that I still feel him peering over my shoulder, eager to offer his views, as I try to write about globalization.

Thomas Hylland Eriksen
Oslo

INTRODUCTION

The very popularity of the word 'globalization' signals a need for caution. The word was scarcely used before the late 1980s, even in academic circles, but today you can hardly open a newspaper without encountering the term. It might easily appear to be a fashionable label used to designate phenomena about which one has only the vaguest ideas. Yet to discard the concept of globalization, and the huge attention accorded the phenomena it encompasses, on such grounds, would be foolish. There is a real need for a common, generic term to describe the manifold, multisided ways in which the world is interconnected, and increasingly so. However, used by itself, the word 'globalization' is empty or at least fuzzy. Before moving to some substantial areas of globalization research in the subsequent chapters of this book, it is therefore necessary to do some sorting and sifting, to delimit some fields of enquiry and to propose a theoretical approach.

The fact that the term globalization is new does not mean that people have not been thinking and theorizing about global interconnectedness before. Perhaps the philosopher Hegel (1770–1831) was the first theorist of globalization, as he did not merely talk of connections between disparate areas and places but about the emerging *consciousness* about such connections. Through his famous concept of the world-spirit (*Weltgeist*) an abstract entity immanent in all peoples but unevenly developed, Hegel saw the possibility of imagining all of humanity as a kind of community. However, Hegel's older contemporary Kant (1724–1804) had already developed, chiefly in his important essay on eternal peace (Kant 2001 [1795]), an idea of cosmopolitanism that entailed equitable and respectful dialogue between the peoples of the world, regardless of their differences. Now, the philosophies of Kant and Hegel were developed in the same period as modern nationalism, and as will later become clear, the ideology of nationalism, although it is often contrasted with and seen as an enemy of globalization, shares many of its characteristics.

The nineteenth century was an era of colonial expansion, scientific discovery and industrialization in the North, and accompanying these processes were new forms of thought, new models of the world. Karl Marx's political philosophy was certainly global in its ambitions, and nineteenth-century cultural historians tended to include all of humanity in their often vast treatises, which usually had an evolutionist bent, placing the author's own society at the top of a developmental ladder. Thanks to industrial development, colonial expansion and technological change (the steamship first appeared in the 1830s), the growth in international trade in that century was formidable. Another important nineteenth-century invention, the telegraph, made it possible, for the first time in human history, to move a message independently of an object physically carrying it. With the opening of the first functioning transatlantic cable in 1866, messages could be sent from London to New York in a matter of minutes. It goes without saying that such innovations changed the perception of space and distance.

Technological development in both main forms of communication technology – that transmitting messages and that transporting physical objects – continued in the twentieth century with the invention of the aeroplane, the radio and so on. In the 1920s, the Marxist theorist Leon Trotsky argued that socialism in one country was impossible since the world was too interconnected for separate development at the national level to be feasible, and agitated in favour of a world revolution. The Second World War was, despite its name, the first truly global war, which involved fighting in, and troops from, all continents (the First World War was chiefly a European war).

In the first post-war decades, global interconnectedness continued to intensify. The number of transnational companies grew, as did the number of transnational NGOs (non-governmental organizations). The United Nations grew into an immense conglomerate of suborganizations with offices in nearly all countries. International travel became easier and more common. In the 1960s, the Canadian media theorist Marshall McLuhan coined the term 'the global village' to designate the new mass media situation, where especially television, in his view, would create shared frames of reference and mutual knowledge between people across the globe (McLuhan 1994 [1964]). In this period, global change – economic, environmental, political – became the subject of many new scholarly books. Some used the term development, intimating that the poor countries would eventually 'catch up with' the rich ones (see, for example, Rostow 1960). Others preferred to use the word 'imperialism', suggesting that the rich countries were actively exploiting the poor ones and preventing them from developing (for example, Frank 1975; Amin 1980). The term 'Westernization', usually used in a derogatory way, became common. Around this time, Immanuel Wallerstein developed his influential world-system theory (Wallerstein 1974–9), which traced the development of the contemporary world system to the intercontinental trade beginning in the fifteenth century. In Wallerstein's view, a permanent international division of labour subsequently developed, dividing the globe into the core (the rich countries), the periphery (the poor countries) and the semiperiphery (countries like Russia, Brazil and China). Elaborating on world-system theory, Chase-Dunn and Hall (1997) take a longer view than Wallerstein, describing the development of transnational systems in a perspective spanning 10,000 years, and showing that a multicentred world was finally becoming integrated at the outset of the nineteenth century, in the sense that all major centres were by then in regular contact. Focusing on cultural processes as well as economic ones, the anthropologist Eric Wolf's *Europe and the People Without History* (Wolf 1982) marked a decisive departure from anthropology's tendency to study ostensibly isolated, small groups. The book, which analyses imperialism from the perspective of the conquered, showed that most 'indigenous' peoples 'stopped being indigenous a long time ago' (Lewellen 2002: 14).

I GLOBALIZATION TODAY

Various parts of the world were interconnected, and there was considerable awareness of this, long before the recent coinage of the term globalization. Yet, it can be argued that there is something new to the present world, that is to say the world which began with the end of the Cold War in 1989–91, which goes a long way to explain the meteoric rise of public interest in globalization and transnational phenomena more generally. Three factors, roughly coinciding in time, may be mentioned here.

- The end of the *Cold War* itself entailed a tighter global integration. The global two-bloc system, which had lasted since the 1940s, had made it difficult to think of geopolitics, transnational communication and international trade in terms not dictated by the opposition between the USA and the Soviet Union and their respective allies. With the dissolution of this conflict, the world seemed to have been left with a one-bloc system (notwithstanding the continued existence of a few states such as North Korea, which continue to stay largely aloof). The world appeared to have become a single marketplace.
- The *Internet*, which had existed in embryonic form since the late 1960s, began to grow exponentially around 1990. Throughout the 1990s, media buzzwords were about bandwidths, Web sites, portals, 'the new economy' and its business opportunities. The World Wide Web was introduced in 1992–3, around the same time as many academics and businesspeople grew accustomed to using e-mail for their daily correspondence. Cellphones became ubiquituous in the rich countries and the middle classes of the poorer ones. The impact of this double delocalization – the physical letter replaced by e-mail, the fixed phone line replaced by the wireless mobile – on the everyday life of millions of people has been considerable, but it remains undertheorized.

- *Identity politics* – nationalist, ethnic, religious, territorial – was at the forefront of the international agenda, both from above (states demanding homogeneity or engaging in ethnic cleansing) and from below (minorities demanding rights or secession). The Salman Rushdie affair, itself an excellent example of the globalization of ideas, began with the issuing of a *fatwa* by Iran's ayatollah Khomeini following the publication of Rushdie's allegedly blasphemous novel *The Satanic Verses* (Rushdie 1988). It soon became apparent that Rushdie could move freely nowhere in the world since the *fatwa* had global implications. Only two years later, Yugoslavia dissolved, with ensuing civil wars based on ethnic differences. In the same period, debates about immigration and multiculturalism came to dominate political discourse in several Western countries, while the Hindu nationalists of the BJP came to power in India.

These three dimensions of globalization – increased trade and transnational economic activity, faster and denser communication networks, increased tensions between (and within) cultural groups due to intensified mutual exposure – do not suggest that the world has been fundamentally transformed after the late 1980s but that the driving forces of both economic, political and cultural dynamics are transnational – and that this is now widely acknowledged. As a pioneering theorist of contemporary globalization, Roland Robertson, succinctly puts it: 'Globalization as a concept refers *both* to the compression of the world *and* the intensification of consciousness about the world as a whole' (Robertson 1992: 8, emphasis mine). The compression of the world, in all of its forms, brings us closer to each other for better and for worse. The consciousness about these interconnections gives a sense of both opportunities and of vulnerability. This dual character of globalization – increased interconnectedness and increased awareness of it – can be studied from a myriad of empirical vantage points. It would be perfectly feasible (and it is probably already being done somewhere) to write a dissertation on European reactions to the Asian bird flu in 2006. The impact of globalization on tribal peoples in Melanesia has, moreover, long been a subject in anthropology. Human geographers write about the displacement of people in India as a result of globally driven economic deregulation. Many write about migration, again from a variety of perspectives. Others are concerned with the distribution of economic power in the global economy, or the distribution of symbolic or definitional power in the global media world; some write about standardization of goods and services as an outcome of the globalization of the economy, others about the spread of certain consumer preferences, yet others about the global tourist industry; while others again study international law, human rights as a consequence of globalization or the 'anti-globalization movement' – just to mention a few subject areas. As far as academic disciplines are concerned, globalization is a central topic in sociology, political science, geography, anthropology, media studies, education, law, cultural studies and so on. The examples in this book, I should emphasize, are meant to indicate variations over a (large) theme and do not claim any form of representativeness.

2 WHAT GLOBALIZATION IS NOT

Before outlining some central analytical dimensions of globalization, it may be a good idea to mention a few things often associated with globalization, either simplistically or wrongly.

- *Globalization is really recent, and began only in the 1980s.* As shown briefly already, this view betrays the beholder's poor knowledge of history. World systems have existed earlier in the sense that people all over the world have participated, often involuntarily, in political and economic systems of a huge, often intercontinental scale. The European colonial era is the most obvious instance but one might argue that the Roman Empire, encompassing as it did most of the known world (for Europeans), or the Aztec Empire, shared many of the characteristics of today's globalization (J. Friedman 1992). However, the inhabitants of such 'world systems' were rarely aware of each other beyond their own experience, and as a form of consciousness, globalization is new as a mass phenomenon. The labour market situation in Oslo has been *known* to thousands of Pakistani villagers for decades, and the reggae fashion in Melanesia, advertising in Central Africa and the rhetoric of the political opposition in Taiwan all indicate the existence of a global *discourse*, a shared (but not uniform) communicational system. In this cultural sense, globalization is recent, and the number of people who are unaware of the existence of television, chewing-gum and basic human rights is decreasing every year.

- *Globalization is just a new word for economic imperialism or cultural Westernization.* This view reduces the vast range of transnational processes to certain economic ones. Although it is tautologically true that rich countries are dominant, the situation is not static. China, India, South Korea and other formerly poor countries are emerging as equal players and regional powers such as South Africa and Brazil are both exploited and exploiters in the global economy. However, the main problem with this view is its neglect of the non-economic dimensions of globalization. The direction of transnational flows is not unilateral: some things flow from north to south, others from south to north, and there is also considerable movement between east and west and within the south. Westernization is not a good synonym for globalization.

- *Globalization means homogenization.* This view is simplistic and usually misleading. First, the participation in global, or transnational, processes often entails a vitalization of local cultural expressions, be it African art, Caribbean popular music or Indian novels, which depend on an overseas market for their survival. Second, large segments of our everyday lives are hardly touched by globalization. Although Taiwanese, like people from the North Atlantic, wear jeans and use iPods while eating burgers and drinking cokes, they do not thereby become Europeans or Americans. However, as will be argued later, it is true that similarities between discrete societies develop as an integral dimension of globalization.

- *Globalization is opposed to human rights.* On the contrary, the global spread of human rights is one of the most spectacularly successful forms of globalization experienced in the world. It is true, of course, that transnational companies operating in poor countries do not necessarily respect workers' rights, but it is only thanks to the globalization of political ideas that local communities and organizations can argue effectively against them and canvas for support from transnational NGOs and governments overseas.

- *Globalization is a threat to local identities.* At the very best this is a truth with serious modifications. As tendencies towards globalization (understood as the dissolution of boundaries) usually lead to strong, localizing counterreactions favouring local food, local customs and so on, some theorists have followed Robertson's (1992) lead in talking about *glocalization* as a more accurate term for what is going on. Local identities are usually strengthened by globalization because people begin to emphasize their uniqueness overtly only when it appears to be threatened. On the other hand, it is evidently true that local *power* is often weakened as a result of globalization. It nonetheless remains indisputable that globalization does not create 'global persons'.

3 GLOBALIZERS AND SCEPTICS

Not everybody who writes about the contemporary world agrees that it has entered a distinctively 'global' era. Some, in fact, argue that the extent of global integration was just as comprehensive, and in some ways more encompassing, in the *belle époque* of 1890–1914 than it is today. Others claim that the nation-state remains, even today, 'the pre-eminent power container of our era' (Giddens, 1985 – he has revised his position since then). Yet others point out that a large number of people, and huge swathes of social and cultural life, are relatively untouched by transnational processes. It may be useful, following Held and McGrew (2000: 38) to distinguish between *globalizers* and *sceptics*, to highlight some of the debates and the positions taken by different scholars.

According to the sceptics (see, for instance, Hirst and Thompson 1999; Gray 2005), we are witnessing a process of *internationalization* and *regionalization* rather than the emergence of *one integrated world* of rapid communication, transnational networks and global financial capital, which is the view of globalizers. Sceptics argue, further, that the nation-state remains the most important political entity, while globalizers claim that state sovereignty is on the wane, and that multilateralism and transnational politics are replacing it. Whereas sceptics have identified the development of regional economic blocs like NAFTA and the EU, globalizers see the world economy as 'a single playing-field' (T. Friedman 2005) with diminishing obstacles to truly global competition. Sceptics see a continuation of the classic North-South divide in terms of prosperity and power, whereas globalizers may argue that inequalities are chiefly growing *within* and not between societies. Sceptics believe in the continued or indeed increasing power of national identities and cultures, but globalizers describe hybridities and cosmopolitan orientations as an outcome of intensified interaction.

The sceptics do not deny that changes are taking place but they emphasize continuities with the modern world of the nation-state whereas globalizers are concerned to show that the world is going through a series of qualitative changes.

There is no reason to take an unequivocal position here. Few of us are simply globalizers or sceptics; and both positions can often shed light on the issues. For example, the extent of global solidarity in environmental and human rights questions is no doubt enhanced by extensive travel and global communication and media, and this lends credibility to the view that cosmopolitanism and cultural hybridity (mixing) results from increased interconnectedness. Yet at the same time, identity politics based on religion, ethnicity or nationality is also on the rise. Both phenomena co-exist side by side and are possible responses to the opportunity space created by intensified transnational contacts. There can be no 'effects' of say, global capitalism, the Internet or politicized Islam, which are not mediated by human understandings and experiences, and they vary. Most empirical generalizations about globalization are therefore false. At the same time, it is possible to delineate a framework for global or transnational processes, objective changes or features of the world to which people everywhere have to relate.

4 DIMENSIONS OF GLOBALIZATION

Whether we look at global capitalism, trends in consumer tastes, transnational migration and identity politics or online communication, the globalizing processes of the late twentieth and early twenty-first centuries have a few salient characteristics in common. These features are dealt with in detail in the main chapters of this book, and I shall only briefly mention them here.

- *Disembedding*, including de-localization. Globalization means that distance is becoming irrelevant, relative or at the very least less important. Ideas, songs, books, investment capital, labour and fashions travel faster than ever, and even if they stay put, their location can be less important than it would have been formerly. This aspect of globalization is driven by technological and economic changes but it has cultural and political implications. Disembedding, however, also includes all manners through which social life becomes abstracted from its local, spatially fixed context.
- *Acceleration*. The speed of transport and communication has increased throughout the twentieth century, and this acceleration continues. It has been said that there are 'no delays any more' in an era of instantaneous communication over cellphones, Internet servers and television satellites. Although this is surely an exaggeration – delays exist, even if only as unintended consequences – speed is an important feature of globalization. Anything from inexpensive plane tickets to cheap calls contribute to integrating the world and the exponential growth in the numbers of Internet users since 1990 indicates that distance no longer means separation.
- *Standardization*. Continuing the processes of standardization begun by nationalism and national economies, globalization entails comparability and shared standards where there were formerly none. The rapid increase in the use of English as a foreign language is suggestive of this development, as is the worldwide spread of, for instance, similar hotels and shopping centres, as well as the growing web of international agreements.
- *Interconnectedness*. The networks connecting people across continents are becoming denser, faster and wider every year. Mutual dependence and transnational connections lead to a need for more international agreements and a refashioning of foreign policies, and create both fields of opportunities, constraints and forms of oppression.
- *Movement*. The entire world is on the move, or so it might sometimes seem. Migration, business travel, international conferences and not least tourism have been growing steadily for decades, with various important implications for local communities, politics and economies.
- *Mixing*. Although 'cultural crossroads' where people of different origins met are as ancient as urban life, their number, size and diversity is growing every day. Both frictions and mutual influence result. Additionally, at the level of culture, the instantaneous exchange of messages characteristic of the

information era leads to probably more cultural mixing than ever before in human history.

- *Vulnerability.* Globalization entails the weakening, and sometimes obliteration, of boundaries. Flows of anything from money to refugees are intensified in this era. This means that territorial polities have difficulties protecting themselves against unwanted flows. Typical globalized risks include AIDS and now avian flu, transnational terrorism and climate change. None can effectively be combated by single nation-states, and it has often been pointed out that the planet as a whole lacks efficient political instruments able to deal with and govern the technology- and economy-driven processes of globalization.

- *Re-embedding.* A very widespread family of responses to the disembedding tendencies of globalization can be described as re-embedding. In fact, all of the seven key features of globalization mentioned above have their countervailing forces opposing them and positing alternatives. The fragmented, fleeting social world made possible through disembedding processes is counteracted through strong networks of moral commitment, concerns with local power and community integration, national and sub-national identity politics.

Moreover, acceleration is counteracted through social movements promoting slowness in many guises, standardization is counteracted by 'one-of-a-kind' goods and services, transnational interconnectedness through localism and nationalism, movement through quests for stability and continuity, mixing through concerns with cultural purity, vulnerability through attempts at self-determination and relative isolation.

Globalization is not a unidirectional process. It has no end and no intrinsic purpose, and it is neither uncontested, unambiguous nor ubiquitous. If we want to see the whole picture, it must include both benefactors and victims, both the globalizers and those who are merely globalized, both those who are caught up in the whirlwind of global processes and those who are excluded. Huge, atrocious slums mushrooming all over the poor parts of the world are products of transnational economic processes, but they are generally seen as the debris of the global economy, the people living there cursorily defined as problems, not resources.

A few further distinctions should also be made initially. The examples in this book deal with economic, political, cultural and environmental aspects of globalization, but the boundaries drawn between such domains are largely artificial and will be dispensed with when they are not needed. It should also be kept in mind that different threads, or domains, in transnational processes do not necessarily move in the same directions, at the same levels of intensity or at the same speed. This means that all societies are unequally affected by different tendencies. Such disjunctures or discrepancies will be explored further.

Globalization can take place, and can be studied, from above or from below. A problematic but necessary distinction, this dichotomy refers to the state, major international organizations and wealthy enterprises on the one hand, and interpersonal relationships on the other hand. I shall argue, and hope to show, that the interpersonal 'globalization from below' is much more encompassing and more important in shaping the world than often assumed.

A distinction between *objective* and *subjective* globalization, also problematic, must be made initially. Objective globalization means being incorporated into a global, or wide-ranging transnational, system without necessarily being aware of it, whereas subjective globalization amounts to the acknowledgement of such processes taking place (which may or may not be occurring: citizens often blame globalization for changes wrought locally).

Finally – and this is a main point in this book – globalization does not entail the production of *global uniformity* or homogeneity. Rather, it can be seen as a way of organizing *heterogeneity*. The similarities dealt with, for example, in the chapter on standardization, are formal and do not necessarily lead to homogeneity at the level of *content*. The local continues to thrive, although it must increasingly be seen as *glocal*, that is enmeshed in transnational processes.

Research on globalization is sprawling and multidisciplinary. It is not the ambition of this book to sum it up, or even to do justice to the vast scope of globalization studies (most of which have been published since 1990). That would plainly have been impossible. Yet it may be kept in mind that much of the research about globalization, and indeed much of the public debate in most countries, is concerned with a few central questions.

First, a chiefly academic question: is globalization new or old? I have already commented briefly on this. The answer has to be sphinxlike: it depends on your definition. Sprawling, but well integrated political systems with thriving trade, internal migration, standardized measures and a common 'high culture' have existed in several continents well before the modern era. However, there are so many characteristic features of our present age, even if we limit it to the post-Cold War era, that it merits treatment on its own terms. One of the leading theorists of the information society, Manuel Castells, confesses, in a lengthy footnote towards the end of his monumental *The Information Age*, that students have sometimes asked him what is new about the world he describes. His answer deserves to be quoted in full:

> Why is this a new world? ... Chips and computers are new; ubiquitous, mobile telecommunications are new, genetic engineering is new; electronically integrated, global financial markets working in real time are new; an inter-linked capitalist economy embracing the whole planet, and not only some of its segments, is new;

a majority of the urban labor force in knowledge and information processing in advanced economies is new; a majority of urban population in the planet is new; the demise of the Soviet Empire, the fading away of communism, and the end of the Cold War are new; the rise of the Asian Pacific as an equal partner in the global economy is new; the widespread challenge to patriarchalism is new; the universal consciousness on ecological preservation is new; and the emergence of a network society, based on a space of flows, and on timeless time, is historically new. (Castells 1998: 336)

A few years later, he could have added the advent of deterritorialized warfare and human-induced climate change to the list. Be this as it may, Castells adds that it does not really matter whether all this is new or not; his point is that this is our world and therefore we should study it.

A second question raised in the debates over globalization, academic and non-academic, concerns the relationship of globalization to neoliberal economics, that is the view that free trade will eventually lead to prosperity everywhere, and that states should encumber the economy as little as possible. Severely criticized (see, for instance, Klein 1998, Gray 1998, Stiglitz 2002, Soros 2002 among very many others) for not delivering the goods – many countries that have complied with measures imposed by international agencies like the World Bank and the International Monetary Fund have experienced a steep decline in *de facto* standards of living – neoliberalism is often associated with, indeed sometimes treated as a synonym for, globalization (Martin and Schumann 1996). Here it must be said that such a usage narrows the concept too much. The global spread of human rights ideas is no less a feature of globalization than the global financial market; the vaccination programmes of the WHO (World Health Organization) are no less global than the moneylending of the World Bank, and the small-scale lending programmes initiated by 2006 Nobel Peace Laureate Mohammad Yunus and his Bangladeshi Grameen Bank have spread to other countries. And so one could go on. Global governance (see the debate in Held et al. 2005) is sometimes posited as an alternative to an anarchic market economy which is in any case imperfect in so far as poor countries rarely obtain full market access in the rich ones. Globalization is form not content; it can be filled with neoliberal market economics, but this is not necessarily happening.

A third, related debate concerns the relationship between globalization and democracy. Many scholars, politicians and commentators are concerned about the loss of political power experienced by nation-states when so much economic power is diverted to the transnational arenas (see, for example, Sassen 1998). Clearly, there are some real issues to be tackled here: the institutions of the nation-state arguably lose some of their clout when capital and wealth are disembedded and become transnational. Yet, the spread of democratic ideas, institutions and practices are also part of the global process. In other words, one cannot say that globalization is either favourable or detrimental to democracy; it is necessary to be more specific.

A fourth, important debate deals with the relationship between poor and rich countries – do the poor become poorer and the rich richer as a result of economic globalization? Again, there can be no simple, unequivocal answer. Who benefits in the long (or for that matter short) run from the globalization of economies? The answer is far from clear. Some countries mired in poverty, notably in Africa, are among the least globalized in terms of integration into the world economy. Their exports are modest, and foreign investment is considered risky and therefore is rare. Some rich countries, not least in Western Europe, begin to notice the competition from poorer countries (notably China and Central-Eastern Europe) as an unpleasant experience. In other cases, it can be argued that current trade regimes, such as the ones negotiated by the World Trade Organization (WTO), help rich countries to continue exploiting poor ones by buying cheap unprocessed goods from them and selling them expensive industrial products back. This would fit with the dependency theory developed by Andre Gunder Frank, Samir Amin and other Marxist scholars, as well as its close relative, Immanuel Wallerstein's world-system theory (see Amin et al. 1982). However, this description fits the older neo-colonial trade regime better than the current one, where China is fast making inroads into markets in Asia and Africa with its inexpensive industrial goods and willingness to invest in industrial enterprises. As argued by Daniel Cohen (2006), the poorest countries are not so much exploited as neglected by transnational investors.

A fifth, no less important theme is that of cultural dynamics: Does globalization lead to homogenization or to heterogenization – do we become more similar or more different due to the increased transnational movement and communication? In one sense, we become more similar. Individualism, which we here take to mean the belief that individuals have rights and responsibilities regardless of their place in wider social configurations, is a central feature of global modernity. It is also easy to argue that similarities in consumer preferences among the world's middle classes indicate 'flattening' or homogenization. Yet at the same time local adaptations of universal or nearly universal phenomena show that global modernities always have local expressions, and that the assumed similarities may either conceal real differences in meaning or that they may be superficial with no deep bearing on people's existential condition. Again, the question is phrased too simplistically to have a meaningful yes/no answer.

Related to this problematic is a sixth area of debate, namely that to do with identity politics. Does globalization, by increasingly exposing us to each other's lives, lead to enhanced solidarity, tolerance and sympathy with people elsewhere; or does it rather lead to ferocious counterreactions in the form of stubborn identity politics

– nationalism, religious fundamentalism, racism and so on? This question has, perhaps, a short answer. Globalization does makes it easier for us to understand each other across cultural divides, but it also creates tensions between groups that were formerly isolated from each other, and it creates a need to demarcate uniqueness and sometimes historical rootedness. The more similar we become, the more different from each other we try to be. Strong group identities may serve several purposes – economic, political, existential – in a world otherwise full of movement and turmoil. Divisive and exclusionary identity politics are a trueborn child of globalization, but so is transnational solidarity.

Finally, an important question concerns how European (or Western, or North Atlantic) globalization is. The conventional view is that globalization is largely fuelled by the economic, technological and political developments of Western Europe. Those who take the long view may begin with the Renaissance, the Italian city-states and the European conquests of the fifteenth and sixteenth centuries; those who write about the present may emphasize transnational corporations, computer technology and the dynamics of capitalism. However, other perspectives may be useful and indeed necessary. If we look at history, the powerhouses of transnational economies have been located in many places. Frank (1998), a long-standing collaborator with Wallerstein, increasingly saw the latter's world-system theory as overly Eurocentric, and showed, in one of his last books, that large-scale transnational markets were flourishing in Asia before and during the European expansionist period, centred on China and parts of India, and leading to both migration waves and cultural exchange. Only with the last period of European colonialization in the nineteenth century did that continent become truly dominant in the world economy, according to Frank. Non-Eurocentric histories of the world, such as Fernandez-Armesto's *Millennium* (1995, cf. also Fernandez-Armesto 2000), also tend to emphasize important interconnections in the past outside Europe. If a Martian were to visit the Earth in the year 1300, Fernandez-Armesto (1995) points out, he would not be able to predict the rise of Europe as the centre of global power. There were thriving civilizations in Mesoamerica, in the Andes, in West Africa, in the Arab world, in India and in China, easily surpassing stagnant European societies in transnational trade, cultural achievements and political might.

If we restrict ourselves to the present, the picture is also less straightforward than a superficial look might suggest. In popular culture as well as literature, major achievements of global significance come from outside the West; Indian films ('Bollywood movies') are popular in many countries, as are Mexican and Brazilian soap operas, Argentine tango and Japanese 'manga' comics. Major alternatives to Western ideologies, such as political Islam, are expanding, and China and India, which combined have 40 per cent of the world's population, have economic growth rates far surpassing those of Western countries. The division of the world into core, periphery and semi-periphery is thus a model that needs to be tested and which does not always yield the expected results.

We shall return to these debates as we go along. Before we move on, I should point out that unlike many introductions to globalization, this book does not suggest *what* to study in the sense of providing a catalogue of substantial topics deemed particularly important by the author. Rather, it suggests *where* to look and to some extent *how* to look for it. The dimensions of globalization presented in the chapters that follow – my key concepts – can be mined for insights through immersion into diverse empirical fields. In the following chapters, I will outline the main characteristics of globalization: It *standardizes, modernizes, deterritorializes* and, by dialectical negation, *localizes* people, because it is only after having been 'globalized' that people may become obsessed with the uniqueness of their locality. I emphasize that although globalization is driven by powerful economic and technological forces, it takes place between people, the transnational webs of the world depend on interpersonal trust, and people often use the opportunities offered by globalizing processes in unexpected ways.

Globalization creates a shared grammar for talking about differences and inequalities. Humans everywhere are increasingly entering the same playing field, yet they do not participate in equal ways, and thus frictions and conflicts are an integral part of globalizing processes. This, too, will be evident in the account that follows.

Chapter Summary

- Globalization entails both the intensification of transnational connectedness and the awareness of such an intensification.
- Globalization is largely driven by technological and economic processes, but it is multidimensional and not unidirectional.
- Globalization entails processes of both homogenization and of heterogenization: it makes us more similar and more different at the same time.
- Globalization is a wider concept than Westernization or neo-imperialism, and includes processes that move from south to north as well as the opposite.
- Although globalization is old in the sense that transnational or even global systems have existed for centuries – indeed for millennia – contemporary globalization has distinctive traits due to enhanced communication technology and the global spread of capitalism.

1 DISEMBEDDING

INTRODUCTION

When, in September 2001, US President George W. Bush announced his 'war on terror', it may have been the first time in history that a war proper was proclaimed on a non-territorial entity. Unlike metaphorical 'wars on substance abuse' or 'wars on poverty', this was meant to be a war fought with real weapons and real soldiers. The only problem was that it initially appeared to be uncertain where to deploy them as terrorism was potentially anywhere. The ostensible goal of the war was not to conquer another country or to defend one's boundaries against a foreign invasion, but to eradicate terrorism, which is a non-territorial entity.

The cause of the declaration of war was the terrorist attack on the US, whereby three civilian airplanes were hijacked by terrorists belonging to the militant Muslim al-Qaeda organization, and flown into the World Trade Center and the Pentagon. A fourth plane, with an uncertain destination, crashed. Rather than seeing this as a horrible crime, the US government defined the event as the beginning of a war. However, it was not to be a war between territorially defined units like nation-states. Several of the hijackers lived and studied in the US. Most of them were of Saudi origins, but they were not acting on orders from the Saudi state. The organization on whose behalf they acted had its headquarters in Afghanistan, but the members were scattered, some living in North America, some in Europe, some in Pakistan and so on.

The nation-state has unambiguous boundaries, it is defined in Anderson's famous terms as being imagined as 'inherently limited and sovereign' (Anderson 1991 [1983]: 6). Wars are fought by the military, whose mission it is to protect the external borders of the country. A nation-state thus has a clearly defined inside and outside. The events of 11 September were a shocking reminder that the boundaries of a nation-state are far from absolute. Nations are effectively being deterritorialized in a number of ways through migration, economic investments and a number of other processes, and the 'war on terror' illustrates that this is now also the case with war. 'America's enemies' can in fact be anywhere in the world and operate from any site, because 'American interests' are global.

A few days after the 11 September events, a thought-provoking photo was reproduced in newspaper worldwide. It depicted military guards watching over the entrances to New York's Grand Central Station. The image was a reminder of two features of globalization: The boundary between police and military becomes blurred even in democracies where the military is not normally visible in the streets and suggests a partial collapse of the boundary between inside and outside. (This blurring of the inside/outside boundary is also evident in the military patrolling of EU borders along the north-west African coast and the military's role in typical transit areas such as the Canary Islands. The division of labour between police and military is negotiable and uncertain in these regions.) Secondly, this image is suggestive of vulnerability in a world society where everything travels more easily than before, including weapons and the people carrying them.

The 'war on terror' is instructive as a lesson in the form of disembedding typical of the global era, where the disembedding mechanisms of modernity, which create abstract common denominators and thus conditions for global communication and comparability, are used transnationally. A main outcome is deterritorialization, that is processes whereby distance becomes irrelevant.

I GLOBALIZATION AND DISTANCE

A minimal definition of globalization could delimit it simply as *all the contemporary processes that make distance irrelevant*. A major body of work in globalization studies is concerned with 'disembedding' (Giddens 1990) and its effects on social life and the organization of society.

This concept (and its close relatives) draws attention to the *relativization of space* engendered by development in communication technologies and the worldwide spread of capitalism. In the early nineteenth-century, newspapers in North America reported from the Napoleonic wars in Europe weeks and sometimes months after the event. News had to be transported by sailships. Travel, even in relatively developed western Europe, was slow, cumbersome and sometimes dangerous. Most goods were, for practical reasons, produced in physical proximity to the markets. With the development of global financial networks, transnational investment capital, consumption mediated by money in all or nearly all societies, and fast and cheap means of transportation, goods can travel, and often do travel, far from their site of production. When it doesn't matter where something was made or done, it has been disembedded.

However, disembedding has a deeper and more comprehensive meaning; it does not merely, or even primarily, refer to the shrinking of the globe as a result of communication technology and global capitalism. Giddens defines disembedding as 'the "lifting out" of social relations from local contexts of interaction and their restructuring across indefinite spans of time-space' (1990: 21). Put in everyday language, it could be described as a gradual movement from the concrete and tangible to the abstract and virtual.

Disembedding processes are associated with modernity and are indeed a central feature of it. Some important disembedding processes evolved in pre-modern times, but the central argument of this chapter is that global modernity, or the globalization of modernity if one prefers, can be described as a series of disembedding processes with a transnational and potentially global reach.

2 TOWARDS A MORE ABSTRACT WORLD

The most important disembedding revolution of pre-modern times was arguably the invention of writing. Through writing, and especially phonetic writing (alphabets rather than pictographies), utterances were separated from the utterer and could, for the first time in human history, travel independently of a given person. The utterance became a permanent, moveable thing. First invented in what is now Turkey, writing was invented independently elsewhere and certainly in Mesoamerica and China. Writing made it possible to develop knowledge in a cumulative way, in the sense that one had access to, and could draw directly on, what others had done. One was no longer dependent on face-to-face contact with one's teachers. They had left their thoughts and discoveries for posterity in a material, frozen form. The quantitative growth in the total knowledge of humanity presupposes the existence of writing. In the thirteenth century a Thomas Aquinas could spend an entire life trying to reconcile two important sets of texts – the Bible and Aristotle's philosophy – which were already considered ancient. Explorers travelling in the Black Sea area in the sixth century AD could compare their observations with Herodotus' descriptions from the fifth century BC. Mathematicians and scientists could use Euclid and Archimedes as points of departure when setting out to develop new insights. Writing makes it possible to stand firmly on the shoulders of deceased and remote ancestors. This would also be the case in other parts of the world with writing systems; Chinese philosophy, Indian mathematics and Mayan astronomy were clearly the result of long, cumulative efforts presupposing a technology capable of freezing thought.

A non-literate society has an oral religion where several versions of the most important myths usually circulate, where the extent of the religion is limited by the reach of the spoken word and where there is no fixed set of dogma to which the faithful must adhere. A literate society, on the contrary, usually has a written religion (often in the shape of sacred texts), with a theoretically unlimited geographic reach, with a clearly delineated set of dogma and principles, and with authorized, 'correct' versions of myths and narratives. Such a religion can in principle be identical in the Arab peninsula and in Morocco (although it is never that simple in practice; local circumstances impinge on it and oral traditions never die completely). The three great religions of conversion from west Asia have all these characteristics, which they do not share with a single traditional African religion. (In real life, nonetheless, oral and literate cultures mix in one and the same societies. The orally transmitted 'little traditions' live side by side with the fixed 'great traditions'.)

A non-literate society, further, has a judicial system based on custom and tradition, whereas a literate society has a legislative system based on written laws. Morality in the non-literate society depends on interpersonal relations – it is embedded in tangible relationships between individuals – whereas morality in the literate society in theory is legalistic, embedded in written legislation. Even the relationship between parents and children is regulated by written law in our kind of society.

In a non-literate society, knowledge is transmitted from mouth to ear, and the inhabitants are forced to train their memories. The total reservoir of knowledge that is available at any particular point in time is embodied in those members of society who happen to be alive. When someone dies in a small, oral society, the net loss of knowledge can be considerable.

Most non-literate societies are organized on the basis of kinship, whereas literate societies tend to be state societies where an abstract ideology of community, such as nationalism, functions as a kind of metaphorical kinship. In certain non-state societies, the 'religions of the Book' have historically worked partly in the same way.

At a political level, the general tendency is that non-literate societies are either decentralized and egalitarian, or chiefdoms where political office is inherited. Literate societies, on the other hand, are strongly centralized, and tend to have a professional administration where office is, in principle, accorded following a formal set of rules. In general, literate societies are much larger, both in geographical size and in population, than non-literate ones. And whereas the inhabitants of non-literate societies tell myths about who they are and where they come from, literate societies have *history* to fill the same functions, based on archives and other written sources.

It should be clear by now that writing has been an essential tool in the transition from what we could call a *concrete society* based on intimate, personal relationships, memory, local religion and orally transmitted myths, to an *abstract society* based on formal legislation, archives, a book religion and written history. I shall mention four other innovations in communication technology, which, together with writing, indicate the extent of disembedding in the social life of modern societies.

3 ABSTRACT TIME AND TEMPERATURE

The mechanical clock was developed in the European Mediaeval age, partly due to a perceived need to synchronize prayer times in the monasteries. (The calls of the Muslim *muezzin* and the Christian church bells are contemporary reminders of this initial function of timing technology.) Calendars are older and were developed independently in many more societies than writing. In general, however, calendars in non-modern societies were not a technical aid to help societies make five-year plans and individuals to keep track of their daily schedules and deadlines, but were rather linked with the seasons, ritual cycles, astronomy and the agricultural year. The clock is more accurate and more minute (literally) than the calendar. It measures time as well as cutting it into quantifiable segments. Despite its initially religious function, the clock rapidly spread to co-ordinate other fields of activity as well. The Dutch thinker Hugo Grotius (1583–1645) formulated a moral maxim that illustrates this. Grotius is widely known for his contributions to political philosophy but he is also sometimes mentioned as the first modern European to defend a moral principle completely divorced from religion: 'Punctuality is a virtue!' ('Time is money' is a later refinement of this principle, sometimes attributed to Benjamin Franklin.)

In the same way as writing externalizes language, clocks externalize time. Time becomes 'something' existing independently of human experience, something objective and measurable. This was definitely not the case in traditional societies, where inhabitants live within an event-driven time structure in their everyday existence. Events regulate the passage of time, not the other way around. If a traveller, or an ethnographer, to an African village wonders when a certain event will take place, the answer may be: 'When everything is ready.' Not, in other words, 'at a quarter to five'. But today, there are no clear-cut distinctions. Even in societies where clocks and timetables made their entry long ago, it may well be that they are not directly connected to people's everyday life. A colleague who carried out anthropological fieldwork in the Javanese countryside told me that one day he needed to take a train to the nearest town. So he asked a man when the train was due. The man looked at him with the proverbial puzzled expression, and pointed to the tracks: 'The train comes from that direction, then it stops here, and after a little while it continues in the other direction.'

Clock time turns time into an autonomous entity, something that exists independently of events. 'An hour' may exist (in our minds) in an abstract way; it is an empty entity that can be filled with anything. Hence it is common to speak of clock time as 'empty, quantified time'. It is chopped up into in accurately measured 'pieces', like metres and decilitres. These entities are presupposed to be identical for everybody, anywhere and any time. Living in our kind of society almost entails that each of us signs a contract the moment we are born, committing us to lifelong faith in clock-and-calendar time.

Mechanical time measurement turns time into an exact, objective and abstract entity, a straitjacket for the ebbs and flows of experienced time perhaps – for this kind of time will always pass at varying speed; as everybody knows, five minutes can be anything from a moment to an eternity. The philosopher who has developed the most systematic assault on this quantitative time tyranny is doubtless Henri Bergson (1859–1941). In his doctoral thesis from 1889, *Sur les données immédiates de la conscience* (*On the Immediate Givens of Consciousness*), rendered in English as *Time and Free Will*, he severely criticizes the quantitative, 'empty' time that regulates us from the outside, instead of letting the tasks at hand fill the time from within.

The clock also has the potential to synchronize everybody who has been brought within its charmed circle. Everyone who reads this is in agreement regarding what it means when we say that it is, say, 8:15 p.m. Everybody knows when to turn on the television to watch a particular programme, and they do it simultaneously, independently of each other. If the programme has already begun when one turns it on, it is not because the TV channel fails to meet its commitments, but because something is wrong with the viewer's timepiece. Co-ordination of complex production in factories and office environments would also, naturally, have been unthinkable without the clock, as would anything from public transport to cinema shows.

The thermometer does the same to temperature as the clock does to time. Under thermometer-driven regimes, it is not acceptable to state merely that it 'feels cold' when one can walk over to the thermometer and obtain the exact number of degrees. If it shows more than 20 degrees Celsius, it is not the air temperature, as it were, but oneself that is to blame.

4 MONEY AS A MEANS OF COMMUNICATION

A more consequential kind of technology than the thermometer is another invention that pulls adherents and victims in the same direction, namely money. In traditional societies, both language and time concepts exist, but not writing and clocks. Similarly, money-like instruments exist in many kinds of societies, but our kind of money, 'general-purpose money', is recent and historically culture-bound. It does roughly the same thing to payment, value measurements and exchange as clocks and writing do to time and language, respectively. They all make the transaction abstract and impose a standardized grid onto a large area (ultimately the whole world). They place individual, mundane transactions under an invisible umbrella of abstraction.

Shell money, gold coins and other compact valuables are known from a wide range of traditional societies. They may, perhaps, be used as value standards to make different goods comparable – a bag of grain equals half a gold coin; a goat equals half a gold coin; *ergo*, a sack of grain can be bartered with a goat. They may be used as means of exchange; I can buy two goats with a gold coin. They may even be used as means of payment – I have killed my neighbour, and I have to pay the widow and children three gold coins in compensation. However, modern money is a much more powerful technology than anything comparable that we know from traditional societies. Above all, it is *universal* in its field of applicability. It may be that Lennon and McCartney were correct in their view that love is not a marketable commodity (although it is easy to find cynical sociologists who argue the contrary), but in general, one single kind of money functions as a universal means of payment and exchange and as a value standard. West African cowries had no value outside a limited area, and even there, only certain commodities and services could be purchased with them. General-purpose money is legal tender in an entire state of millions of inhabitants and, if we belong to a country with a convertible currency, they are valid worldwide. Regarded as information technology, money has truly contributed to the creation of one world, albeit a world into which only people of means are integrated. Money makes wages and purchasing-power all over the world comparable, makes it possible to exchange a tonne of taro from New Guinea with electronics from Taiwan, and it is a necessary medium for the world economy to be possible at all. Whereas transaction and trade in many societies depended on trust and personal relationships between seller and buyer, the abstract and universal money we are familiar with imply an externalization of economic transactions. As long as there is agreement over the economic value of the coloured bits of paper I need not know either my debtors or my creditors personally. With the recent move of money into cyberspace, which entails that the same plastic card can be used for economic transactions nearly anywhere in the world, it becomes even more abstract.

5 ABSTRACT MUSIC

A final example is musical notation. Most (all?) societies we know possess some kind of music, but notation was only invented a couple of times, namely in Europe (ninth century AD) and China/Japan (tenth century AD). However, it was only in Europe that an expressed aim of notation from the very beginning was to create an entirely symbolic language for communicating musical content – the Chinese/Japanese system was based on pictographs proper to the written language. In the beginning, the rudimentary notes marked only ascent and descent of tone level. Eventually, they became more accurate, and in the eleventh century, Guido of Arezzo introduced the staff, which made it possible to mark specified intervals. In the same period, the notation system was standardized, and symbolic markers depicting tone duration were also introduced. At the beginning of the sixteenth century, the system with which we are familiar was largely in place.

Several aspects of musical notation are relevant in the present context. First, written music do the same to music as script does to language; they liberate music from the performer and make it possible to store music independently of people and allow for individual players to learn a piece without personal contact with another performer. Only those aspects of music that can be depicted in writing are copied with a high degree of fidelity across the generations. Just as there is an indefinite residue in speech that is not transmitted through texts, the same could be said of music (feeling and, for a long time, speed, are two such aspects). Secondly, notes freeze music, just as history freezes myths and clock time attempts to fix the variable flow of time. In several European countries, folk music that had evolved gradually for centuries was suddenly transcribed and preserved in frozen form during national romanticism; as a result, it is played today note by note as it was played, say, in the mid-nineteenth century (Sinding-Larsen 1991). Thirdly, notation lays the conditions for another kind of complexity than what would otherwise have been possible. Tellingly, notation was developed in the same period as polyphony, a musical innovation that appeared

---

The Gated Community as a Form of Disembedding

Segregation in cities has been studied widely by urban sociologists, anthropologists and not least geographers. The term 'gated community', often used in the literature, describes an urban area that is guarded, usually by a private security company, and closed off, usually physically, from the surrounding city. The people inhabiting the gated community are economically privileged, and have closed off their local area in order to control their interaction with the surroundings, seen as threatening and dangerous. Naturally, the gated community is a feature of cities that are strongly class divided. Inhabitants of the gated community have their own infrastructure, wholly or partially, they send their children to private schools and buy imported goods in expensive shops. In an analysis of the development of a gated community, or fortified enclave, in Managua, Nicaragua, Rodgers (2004: 123) describes them as 'disconnected worlds that are the antithesis of public space, in that they constitute a withdrawal from the fabric of the city, leading to its fragmentation.' The social form of the gated community leads to the exclusion of others from formerly shared spaces, and limits the interaction between the enclave's inhabitants and outsiders. It definitely contributes to a fragmentation of the city and also has consequences for the political life in that the very notion of a shared public space is

only in Europe. Neither the mathematical regularity of Bach's fugues nor the very large number of voices in Beethoven's symphonies would have been possible without an accurate system of notation. The standard tone A440 (a pure A is a wave with the frequency 440) was finally defined in 1939, after having fluctuated for hundreds of years. It is the equivalent in music to the gold standard, Greenwich Mean Time and the metre rod in France. A shared, abstract standard is assumed to be valid for all persons at all times.

6 WATERSHEDS

The transitions from kinship to national identity, from custom to legislation, from 'cowrie money' or similar to general-purpose money, from local religions to written religions of conversion, from person-dependent morality to universalistic morality, from memory to archives, from myths to history, and from event-driven time to clock time, all point in the same direction: from a small-scale society based on concrete social relations and practical knowledge to a large-scale society based on an abstract legislative system and abstract knowledge founded in logic and science.

Two further historical changes, with important implications for both thought and ways of life, need mentioning as conditions for widespread disembedding: printing and the industrial revolution.

---

challenged. Inhabitants of gated communities consume pretty much in the same way as middle or upper class citizens in rich countries; they watch cable television and communicate online from home. Their integration into the world economy is indisputable — many work in international agencies or transnational companies — but their level of participation in the domestic public sphere is debatable and often very insignificant. The spread of gated communities throughout the poorer countries — Rio de Janeiro, Nairobi, Johannesburg, Santiago de Chile, Guatemala City and so on — suggests not only a disembedding of an urban form from its physical location but also the emergence of a global middle class, transnationally integrated through shared ideas, practices and lifestyles, but with a weakening tie towards the local and domestic.

This example suggests a development that is complementary to, and signifies the opposite of, the example of the fourteenth Chilean province (see pp. 28–29). Whereas the Internet and increased transnational interaction can serve to reintegrate diaspora Chileans into the imagined community of the nation, the growth of gated communities in Third World cities signifies the detachment from the nation-state of groups that are physically located in it.

Before the era of print – Johann Gutenberg lived from about 1400 to 1468 – literacy existed in many societies but it was not particularly widespread. There were several causes for this – among other things, the fact that a book could be as costly as a small farm. Books were always written by hand, largely by monks, but also by professional copyists. Then Gutenberg invented his printing press, frequently seen as the single most important invention of the last two thousand years and, suddenly, books became inexpensive. From 1455 and onwards, to be exact; this was the year Gutenberg printed the famous 42-line Bible. Books did not become really cheap immediately. Gutenberg's Bible cost thirty guilders, and the annual salary for a worker was ten guilders. During the following decades, the new technology spread to cover the central parts of Europe and books became increasingly inexpensive. The first printing shop in England was founded by William Caxton in 1476. Caxton was printer, editor, book salesman and publisher (a common combination as late as the nineteenth century) and he contributed in no small degree to standardizing English orthography and syntax. Printing entailed standardization in other countries too, as well as facilitating access to books written in native languages, at the expense of Latin. The market was suddenly much larger than the small elite of Latin scholars. Printing was a decisive factor for the emergence of new science, philosophy and literature in early modern times. It was crucial for both mass education and the creation of civil society in European cities, and led to consequences that Gutenberg could never have foreseen. His main ambitions seem to have been to print Bibles and pay his debts.

The features of printing that are most relevant here are its contribution to the spectacular growth in information and its standardizing effects on language and thought. Cheap, printed books contributed to the standardization of both language and worldviews. An identical message, clothed in identical linguistic garb, could now be broadcast to the entire middle class from Augsburg to Bremen. Thus a national public sphere could emerge for the first time, consisting of equals who were preoccupied with the same writers, the same political and theological questions, the same philosophical, geographic and scientific novelties. Printing was so important for the development of democracy and nationalism that Benedict Anderson gave the leading role to print capitalism in his historical drama about the rise of nationalism, *Imagined Communities* (Anderson 1991 [1983]). Without this formidable system of production and distribution, it is difficult to see how a person in Marseilles could even dream of having a morally committing feeling of community with a person in Lille. Seen as a technological device for creating abstract communities, that is solidarity and empathy between people who will never meet in the flesh, print capitalism is king. An underlying question for us is, naturally: if print capitalism bequeathed nationalism and democracy, what lies in store for us after a period similarly dominated by the Internet and digital satellite television?

It took a long time for literacy to become truly widespread even after the rise of printing technology. In Shakespeare's time, perhaps 10 per cent of the population in England and Wales was literate. No country has an illiteracy rate even approaching this today. Even women in conservative, patriarchal societies have a higher literacy rate than the citizens of Shakespeare's England.

It was printing coupled with universal primary education and mass media like newspapers and magazines (including books published in monthly instalments) that truly pulled the minds of ordinary men and women into the new, abstract society. This society consisted of an enormous number of persons who were all cogs in a giant machine, and eventually they could easily be replaced by others in the productive process. Their knowledge and skills were not unique but standardized and therefore comparable to others' knowledge and skills. With the industrial revolution in the nineteenth century, this possibility was turned into practice for the first time.

7 NATIONALISM AS A TEMPLATE FOR GLOBALIZATION

Nationalism, often seen as an obstacle to globalization, is a product of the same forces that are shaping the latter (see Sassen 2006 for the full argument). Historically, an important part played by nationalist ideologies in contemporary nation-states has been to integrate an ever larger number of people culturally, politically and economically. The French could not be meaningfully described as a 'people' before the French revolution, which brought the Ile-de-France (Parisian) language, notions of liberal political rights, uniform primary education and not least, the self-consciousness of being French, to remote areas – first to the local bourgeoisies, later (in some cases *much* later) to the bulk of the population. Similar large-scale processes took place in all European countries during the nineteenth century, and the modern state, as well as nationalist ideology, is historically and logically linked with the spread of literacy (Goody 1986), the quantification of time and the growth of industrial capitalism. The model of the nation-state as the supreme political unit has spread throughout the twentieth century. Not least due to the increasing importance of international relations (trade, warfare and so forth), the nation-state has played an extremely important part in the making of the contemporary world. Social integration on a large scale through the imposition of a uniform system of education, the introduction of universal contractual wagework, standardization of language and so forth are accordingly the explicit aim of nationalists in, for instance, contemporary Africa. It is, of course, possible to achieve this end through contrasting the nation with a different nation or a minority residing in the state, which is then depicted as inferior or threatening. This strategy for cohesion is extremely widespread and is not a peculiar characteristic of the nation-state as such: similar ideologies and practices are found in kinship-based societies and among urban minorities alike. Insofar as enemy projections are dealt with in the present context, they are regarded as means to achieve internal, national cohesion, since international conflicts are not considered.

Nationalism as a mode of social organization represents a qualitative leap from earlier forms of integration. Within a national state, all men and women are citizens, and they participate in a system of relationships where they depend upon, and contribute to, the existence of a vast number of individuals whom they will never know personally. The main social distinction appears as that between insiders and outsiders; between citizens and non-citizens. The total system appears abstract and impenetrable to the citizen, who must nevertheless trust that it serves his needs. The seeming contradiction between the individual's immediate concerns and the large-scale machinations of the nation-state is bridged through nationalist ideology proposing to accord each individual citizen particular value. The ideology simultaneously depicts the nation metaphorically as an enormous system of blood relatives or as a religious community and as a benefactor satisfying immediate needs (such as education, jobs, health and security). Through this kind of ideological technique nationalism can serve to open and close former boundaries of social systems. Some individuals become brothers metaphorically; others, whose citizenship (and consequently, loyalty) is dubitable, become outsiders. Unlike in pre-modern societies, nationalism communicates mainly through abstract media (written laws, newspapers, mass meetings etc.) whereas kinship ideology is communicated in face-to-face interaction. The former presupposes the latter as a metaphoric model (Eriksen 2002, see also Smith 1991).

Nationalism is ideally based on abstract norms, not on personal loyalty. Viewed as a popular ideology, nationalism is inextricably intertwined with the destiny of the nation-state. Where the nation-state is ideologically successful, its inhabitants become nationalists; that is, their identities and ways of life gradually grow compatible with the demands of the nation-state and support its growth. Where nationalism fails to convince, the state may use violence or the threat of violence to prevent fission. The monopoly on the use of legitimate violence is, together with its monopoly of taxation, one of the most important characteristics of the modern state; however, violence is usually seen as a last resort. More common are political strategies aiming to integrate hitherto distinctive categories of people culturally. Since national boundaries change historically, and since nations can be seen as shifting collectivities of people conceiving of their culture and history as shared, this is an ongoing process. Ethnic groups can vanish through annihilation or more commonly, through assimilation. They may also continue to exist, and may pose a threat to the dominant nationalism in two main ways, either as agents of subversion (they do, after all, represent alternative cultural idioms and values – this was how the Jews of Nazi Germany were depicted) or as agents of fission (which was evidently the case with Baltic nationalists before 1991).

Nationalist strategies are truly successful only when the state simultaneously increases its sphere of influence, and responds credibly to popular demands. It is tautologically true that if the nation-state and its agencies can satisfy perceived needs in ways acknowledged by the citizens, then its inhabitants become nationalists. The main threats to national integration are therefore alternative social relationships, which can also satisfy perceived needs. There are potential conflicts between the nation-state and non-state modes of organization, which may follow normative principles incompatible with those represented by the state. This kind of conflict is evident in every country in the world, and it can be studied as ideological conflict, provided ideology is not seen merely as a system of ideas but as sets of practices guided by such ideas. Typical examples are African countries, where 'tribalism' or organization along ethnic lines is perceived as a threat (by the nation-state), or as an alternative (by the citizens), to the universalist rhetoric and practices of nationalism. From the citizen's point of view, nationalism may or may not be a viable alternative to kinship or ethnic ideology (or there may be two nationalisms to choose between, such as an Ethiopian and a Somali one in eastern Ethiopia) – and she will choose the option best suited to satisfy her needs, be they of a metaphysical, economic or political nature. The success or failure of attempts at national integration must therefore not only be studied at the level of political strategies or systemic imperatives; it must equally be understood at the level of the everyday life-world. The ideological struggles and the intra-state conflicts, as well as the context-specific options for 'the good life', shape and are simultaneously rooted in the immediate experiences of its citizens, and the analysis must begin there.

8 OTHER DISEMBEDDING MECHANISMS

In the realm of production, the *labour contract* of the capitalist enterprise was a disembedding instrument separating the labour power of the individual from the entire person. Under a labour contract, workers were and are, at least in principle, free to quit, and their obligations to the employer are limited to their working hours. Other examples could have been added. The point is that modern societies are characterized by a particular kind of complexity. It is not the only one possible.

Indian caste society and traditional Australian worldviews are two spectacular examples of social and cultural complexity, respectively. Nonetheless, modernity is today in a uniquely important position; it is hegemonic on the verge of becoming universal. It synchronizes and standardizes an enormous number of persons, all of them little cogs in a great machinery. It draws on a shared mechanical time structure, a global medium for economic transactions (money), technologies of production and destruction based on a shared theoretical science and easily transferrable knowledge. Modernity co-ordinates the movements and thoughts of an enormous number of people in ways which were both unknown and unthinkable in non-modern societies. It divorces its resources from particular individuals by externalizing time, language, economy, memory, morality and knowledge. And it lays the foundation for a nearly infinite social complexity in a world where boundaries are increasingly relative and negotiable.

So far, I have considered some of the main conditions of modernity, chiefly in its guise as the modern nation-state. However, with the replication and diffusion of technologies and modes of organization across boundaries, what emerged during the twentieth century, and particularly in its second half, was a world system of nation-states based on many of the same premises. Thus, given these emerging similarities across the globe, contemporary globalization became feasible. It would neither be economically profitable nor culturally possible to create enduring ties between non-state, non-literate tribal groups and the economic machinery of the industrialized

The Fourteenth Chilean Province

Disembedding means the 'lifting out' of social relations from their local embeddedness. Thinking along these lines, and looking at identification and belonging, one might imagine the development of state-sponsored virtual nations on the Internet, ensuring the continued loyalty and identification of citizens or ex-citizens living abroad. In terms of economics and strategic interests, such an enlarging of the national interest, this makes perfect sense. The Chilean government discovered this potential in the early 2000s. During the military dictatorship (1973–1990), roughly a million Chileans left the country, and the majority did not return after the reintroduction of democracy. There are people registered as Chileans in 110 countries around the world, even if many lost their citizenship after fleeing from the Pinochet dictatorship.

In recent years, the government has actively sought to reintegrate overseas Chileans and their descendants, not by encouraging their return, but by enhancing their sense of Chileanness, which might in turn benefit the state through investments and 'Chilean' activities scattered around the globe. Chile is officially made countries, but with the increasingly transnational disembedding of communication, trade and production, such ties have become both viable and widespread.

Giddens (1990) distinguishes between two kinds of disembedding mechanisms: the creation of *symbolic tokens*, and the establishment of *expert systems*. A typical symbolic token is money, which travels independently of persons and goods (and is increasingly located to the abstract realm of cyberspace); a typical expert system is economic science, assumed to be context-independent and valid everywhere.

As has been mentioned, the increasing dominance of disembedding mechanisms and their growing spatial range can fruitfully be seen as a movement from the concrete to the abstract, from the interpersonal to the institutional and from the local to the global. The two next chapters, on acceleration and on standardization, present features of globalization which are closely related to disembedding.

9 CRITICS OF DISEMBEDDING

An especially grim interpretation of disembedding processes sees them as resulting in fragmentation and anonymity, ultimately removing every trace of the local and particular. In an original essay on 'non-places', the anthropologist Marc Augé (1992) describes a condition he labels 'supermodernity' (*la surmodernité*), which continuously produces uprootedness and alienation because it lacks historically rooted places imbued with particularity. Augé's non-places are frictionless and lack

---

up of thirteen regions, but increasingly, a fourteenth region, called the region of *el exterior* or *el reencuentro* (the reunion) is mentioned in official and unofficial contexts. The Chilean government's Web site (www. gobiernodechile.cl) has a first-order link to a subsite called 'Chilenos en el exterior', and there has been talk of giving voting rights to Chileans abroad. Initiatives have even been taken to allow Chilean artists living abroad to apply for government funding.

The use of the Internet by states in order to stimulate and kindle national loyalty among nationals living in diasporas may become both widespread and controversial in the near future. Given that most debates about immigration in the receiving countries deal with integration, this kind of measure is bound to be perceived as a fragmenting force in the host countries. Yet, disembedding mechanisms, of which the Internet is one, have the potential of making political boundaries congruent with cultural ones, as Ernest Gellner puts it in *Nations and Nationalism* (Gellner 1983) – even when both kinds of boundaries are thoroughly deterritorialized.

resistance. They communicate through a rudimentary pidgin language devoid of particular experiences. He writes that we live in a world where one is

> born in a clinic and dies in a hospital, where transitional points – luxurious or dehumanising – proliferate (hotel chains and temporary shacks, holiday resorts, refugee camps, slums soon to be demolished or which are in a condition of permanent decay), where a network develops which is tied together by means of transportation which are also dwellings, where the routine user of shopping centres, ATMs and credit cards carries out his transactions without a word, a world where everything encourages lonely individuality, the transition, the provisional and temporary. (Augé 1992: 100–1, my translation)

In the abstract, generalized world described by Augé, the local and peculiar is lost. Augé's countryman Paul Virilio (1996, 2000) goes even further, in seeing disembedding processes as heralding the death of civil society. In Virilio's view, a main cause of social fragmentation and alienation is contemporary communication technology. Whereas some of the disembedding communication technologies, notably the book and the newspaper, were important for the creation of civil societies by creating shared frames of reference for people who would never meet physically (Anderson 1991 [1983]), the contemporary, transnational and instantaneous communication technologies (such as the Internet) dissolve it in Virilio's view. He describes a world where people no longer need to – or even want to – meet their neighbours, where they are entertained and informed online, and where communication with others is also increasingly online, deterritorialized, disembedded and detached from ongoing social life. As a result, Virilio fears that the everyday conversation about society, the little compromises and conversions taking place in discussions about anything from sport to politics, fade away because the organization of society no longer creates conditions for such interactions.

There is, in the social sciences, a long tradition of criticizing modern societies, and not least the features that we have described as disembedding processes, for alienating people and reducing the conditions for existential security, intimacy, self-reliance and autonomy. Most of the leading pioneers of social theory, including Marx, Durkheim and Tönnies, contrasted the abstract, large-scale, industrial societies of their own day with the concrete, small-scale, agricultural societies that had preceded them. Some of their arguments can be re-found in contemporary debates about globalization, which is in a certain sense just modernity writ large or, in the words of Appadurai (1996), simply *modernity at large*. However, the era of global modernity is in important ways different from the modernity defined and described by the sociological classics. Notably, the economy and communications have become increasingly globalized – or deterritorialized – without a similar development in politics. The 'democratic deficit' of globalization is a much-debated topic (cf. Held et al. 2005), and in the view of the critics, the national public and political spheres are being marginalized. Some call for a strengthening of national power, whereas others argue in favour of transnational governance through international organizations and regional entities like the European Union. Yet others have faith in the potential of 'grassroots' movements – that is organizations from below – as alternative ways of influencing both local and transnational politics.

By presenting some of the disembedding mechanisms of modernity at some length, this chapter has shown how contemporary globalization is a development presupposing the implementation and dissemination of a series of disembedding processes, which have created abstract societies, now increasingly transnational in their ongoings.

Chapter Summary

- Disembedding can be defined as 'the 'lifting out' of social relations from local contexts of interaction and their restructuring across indefinite spans of time-space'.
- Disembedding refers to a main trajectory of globalization, namely the increasingly abstract character of communication and objects, whereby their origin becomes obscured and their currency more and more widespread.
- Writing (often in the form of printing), money, clock time and standardized measurements are some of the most important disembedding mechanisms in modern society.
- The disembedding mechanisms of contemporary global or transnational systems rely on electronic information and communication technology (ICT) for their efficacy.
- Critics of contemporary disembedding see the 'lifting out' of social relations as a recipe for alienation and fragmentation.

2 ACCELERATION

As a result of the need for instantaneous responses, particularly because of the speed implied by the telephone, telex, fax, electronic signals and so on, the future increasingly appears to dissolve into an extended present.

John Urry, *Sociology Beyond Societies*

And far too many suffer from chronic image flicker, a synchronic experience of reality as images rich in details, not as lines across time, causal chains, reasoning. One needs both, but the way it is today, the ability to think is slowly killed, to the advantage of the ability to see and hear, taste and feel – a orgy of the senses that gives little space for intellectuality.

Johan Galtung, *Johan uten land* (my translation)

INTRODUCTION

As I sat by my desk in relative peace and quiet a fine spring morning some years ago I was interrupted by three simultaneous and identical e-mails marked with red tags ('Priority: High!'), followed by a physical visit by the secretary, who actually walked around in the corridor, knocking doors and warning the occupants of imminent danger. After we got e-mail in the early 1990s, we hardly saw the secretary any more, and so we immediately understood that the situation had to be very serious.

Now, the reason for this unusual and dramatic behaviour was neither a fire on the first floor, a general strike, an attempted coup d'etat by the military or even a spontaneous wave of suicides among university employees protesting against the decay of our institution, but a small computer program that had settled on many of our hard disks. A virus! The virus program had arrived as an attachment to an e-mail entitled 'ILOVEYOU', which contained an imploring request for the recipient to open the attached 'love letter from me to you'. If one did – and many did, understandably, given that they had been promised an unconditional declaration of love – a malign virus would begin deleting files, messing up data and then proceed to move on to other innocent computers via the victim's electronic address list. A surprising number of colleagues received the virus before lunch on that day, generally from different sources, and many got it twice or even three times.

The virus, which in a matter of hours had been nicknamed 'The Love Worm', was first observed in Hong Kong late in the evening on Wednesday, 3 May 2000 (local time). When the American population began to get out of bed a little while later (and it was Wednesday morning in the US), the virus began to move across the world with astonishing speed. Within the next couple of days it had settled – among many other places – at the University of Gothenburg, a weekly Oslo newspaper and the Norwegian Institute of International Studies, and arrived from individual computers in all three places to my computer on Thursday morning. As people began to return home from work on that fateful Thursday, the leading anti-virus companies had already developed remedies that were freely available on the Web. The virus was virulent and epidemic from the very beginning (other, real-world viruses, such as that which carries bubonic plague, may be endemic for years before turning vicious), and the entire epidemic lasted less than three days. Within that span, between 60 per cent and 80 per cent of the computers in the US were estimated to have been infected to a greater or lesser degree. On Thursday evening, the CNN online reported that the Scandinavian photo agency Scanpix had lost 4,500 images, despite impeccable security routines.

A couple of days' later the epidemic dissemination all over the world was brought to an abrupt end, following the spread of loud warnings in virtually all the world's media. A week later, the virus makers were arrested by the Filipino police.

One cannot help but compare this epidemic with earlier major epidemics in European history. The most famous and most consequential was the Black Death (1347–51). It had already caused mass death and political fragmentation in large parts of Europe for a couple of years when it finally reached Bergen in 1349, arriving in the Baltic lands only the following year. It took the plague three years to make the trip from Sicily to Riga, in spite of being extremely contagious. Excepting the immediate neighbouring areas (West Asia and North Africa), no other continents than Europe were affected. Indeed, the great plague of the 530s (Keys 1999) was more global – it started in East Africa and wrought havoc in China, Arabia and Europe – and it moved just as fast as the plague eight hundred years later. Whatever was far away in space, in the fourteenth century as well as in the sixth, was also far removed in time.

Acceleration is a central feature of globalization and indeed of modernity. Everything, it seems, happens faster and faster, bringing disparate parts of the world closer to each other.

1 TIME-SPACE COMPRESSION

The concept of disembedding discussed in the previous chapter refers chiefly to the reorganization of social relations by virtue of processes which render society and culture more abstract and detached from local circumstances. Although disembedding is a key feature of modernity itself, it was argued that it is also an important condition for stable transnational connections and globalization, since it makes things, people and ideas more easily comparable and moveable than they were, and are, in societies where most of what goes on is embedded in the local.

A close relative to Giddens' concept of disembedding is the geographer David Harvey's term 'time-space compression', developed in Harvey's important book *The Condition of Postmodernity* (Harvey 1989). You may envision it as the squeezing together of time and space. The aspects of deterritorialization briefly discussed in the context of disembedding are also instances of time-space compression. There are many possible theoretical approaches to our near past, and the history of modernity has kept generations of academics and students busy for more than a century. Some concentrate on the history of ideas whereas others emphasize economics or politics. It can be done differently. For example, it can be highly illuminating to view the history of the last 200 years as a history of acceleration. Strangely, this dimension is rarely foregrounded in the extensive literature on globalization. The reason why this should come as a surprise, is simply that globalization is tantamount to a particular form of acceleration, which reduces the importance of distance, frequently obliterating it altogether. In the era of wireless communications, there is no longer a connection between duration and distance. In 1903, Theodore Roosevelt sent a round-the-world telegram to himself, and it reached him in nine minutes (Anderson 2005: 3). Today, such an exercise would not have made sense, but a century ago it indicated that the world had become a smaller place, the space–time continuum had been compressed enormously compared with the situation only half a century earlier, when there was no way Roosevelt could have sent a telegram even to London.

Technological changes are necessary conditions for time-space compression. The jet plane and the satellite dish automatically enable people to communicate fast in both senses of the word, but their mere invention says nothing about their social importance; who has access to these technologies, how are they being used, how do they contribute to transforming economies and everyday lives worldwide. When we study technological changes, therefore, they must always be placed in their social context. One of the most interesting findings in the interdisciplinary research on information and communication technologies is that they have hugely different social implications and cultural connotations in different societies.

Harvey defines time-space compression like this:

> [P]rocesses that so revolutionize the objective qualities of space and time that we are forced to alter, sometimes in quite radical ways, how we represent the world to ourselves. I use the word 'compression' because a strong case can be made that the history of capitalism has been characterized by speed-up in the pace of life, while so overcoming spatial barriers that the world sometimes seems to collapse inwards upon us. (Harvey 1989: 240)

This 'speed-up' is then illustrated graphically (Harvey 1989: 241) by looking at four maps of the world indicating the fastest available transport technology at the time:

1. 1500–1840 (best average speed of horse drawn coaches and sailing ships was 10 m.p.h.);
2. 1850–1930 (steam locomotives averaged 65 m.p.h. and steam ships averaged 36 m.p.h.);
3. 1950s (propeller aircraft, 300–400 m.p.h.);
4. 1960s (jet passenger aircraft, 500–700 m.p.h.).

A similar list showing the acceleration in the communication of messages would be no less striking, but less tidy. For hundreds, indeed thousands of years, the fastest widespread means of communication was the written document, transported by a horse (trained pigeons were unusual). Intercontinental communication could take place no faster than a sail ship. With the coming of the train and steamship in the early decades of the nineteenth century, the speed of communication increased as much as the speed of ground communication; however, long before the steamboats had fully replaced sail ships, a momentous innovation saw the light of day, namely the telegraph, which was first demonstrated in 1838. For the first time in history, a message could be transported without being embedded in a physical object. The first transatlantic cable between New York and London was opened in 1866; the first cable from London to Bombay in 1870. Although the telegraph was used chiefly for short messages, transmitted in Morse code (now obsolete but learnt routinely by boy scouts as late as the 1980s), it revolutionized the way people experienced time and space. Suddenly, a remote city could be experienced as very near if it was connected by cable; similarly, towns or villages in the neighbourhood appeared to be remote if they were uncabled. The train and the telephone (invented in 1877) similarly contributed to changing the time-space continuum. As from the late nineteenth century, one could no longer draw on an intuitive connection between distance and delay. Some towns and cities were connected fast through ground transportation, instantaneously through the telegraph and telephone.

2 ACCELERATED CHANGE

As one the most important theorists of speed, Paul Virilio, likes to say: 'We now live in an era with no delays.' Virilio has the Internet family of technologies in mind and thus he is not overstating the point. (It should be quite clear that he is neither thinking of commuter trains into London nor of citizens waiting to speak to a civil servant on the phone.) Global telecommunications and other communication based on satellites are placeless and immediate. All the nodes connected through the Internet are in reality both in the same place, everywhere and nowhere. In practice, there is no difference between sending and receiving e-mail from Melbourne or from the office next door; or watching a direct transmission from a football game in Belgium, New Year celebrations in Kiribati or an interview transmitted from one's local television studio. Time, regarded as a means to create distance and proximity, is gone.

This familiar fact has many unintended consequences, some of which are explored by Virilio, who talks of his own field of study as *dromology*, the study of speed and acceleration. One of his special fields of interest is the military. At the outset of the twentieth century it would take weeks or months to invade a country like Poland. The speed of war was identical with the average speed of the cavalry. Although horses are fast animals, they need food and rest, and they are further delayed by hills, swamps and rivers – not to mention intransigent villagers who are liable to destroy bridges and set traps. At the beginning of the last century, the tank and the double-decker airplane were introduced, and suddenly the speed of war was increased several times. Then came the Spitfires and medium-range missiles, and today a warlike state can in principle inflict unspeakable damage on another country in a matter of minutes.

Technologies spread faster and faster. It took forty years for radio to gain an audience of 50 million; in the case of personal computers, the figure was fifteen, and only four years after its introduction in 1992, fifty million people were using the World Wide Web. As I write in 2007, the number hovers around a billion. This is impressive, but still, only one in six humans have access to the Internet, meaning that its dissemination is uneven. The total number of Internet users in sub-Saharan Africa, excepting South Africa, is lower than that of Finland.

However, the new technologies also spread to new areas. In the late 1990s, text messages were unknown in China. In 2006, between twelve and fourteen *billion* text messages were sent every month in the same country.

In a widely read book about globalization published in 2005, Thomas Friedman refers to one of his earlier books, published back in 1999, by saying that the globalization processes that interests him were just beginning back then. Speaking of contemporary globalization as 'Globalization 3.0', Friedman argues forcefully that only in the first years of the twenty-first century, momentous changes have led to a much more integrated, 'flatter' world than the world of even the last decade of the twentieth century. One may shrug at this generalization – Friedman's most convincing defence of the view is the commonplace that China's economic impact on the world has grown tremendously and very fast – but his view illustrates a widespread feeling, not altogether unjustified, that changes are happening quickly.

Friedman mentions ten 'flatteners' which have each contributed to 'levelling the playing field'. All of them are to do with information and communication technology and with acceleration, ranging from the explosion in twenty-four hour parcel delivery (the UPS fleet is now the eleventh largest airline in the world) and broadband connections to computerized logistics on a huge scale. Software developers in India, he notices, no longer have to move to the US to have a career because their geographical location is unimportant. He also describes the Wal-Mart supply chain in some detail, showing how it profits from deterritorialized markets and remarking that, if Wal-Mart had been a country, it would have been China's eighth largest trading partner! Friedman tells many other stories in his readable book, of innovators dreaming up new products, cutting prices or speeding up production or distribution, all of them involving computers in one way or another. Partly Friedman's evolutionist scheme (he really believes that the world is moving in one direction) is like an undialectical form of Marxism – a Marxism without conflict – and partly it is an extension of the theory of industrial society developed by sociologists and economists in the twentieth century. What is new is global simultaneity under informational capitalism.

In the domains of information technology, consumption and retail trade, the world is doubtless becoming 'flatter', to use Friedman's term, although it should be kept in mind that perhaps half the world's population does not take part in this. If we look at acceleration from a spatial point of view, it becomes evident that certain places change much faster than others. The central nodes of any disembedded activities are characterized by a much higher speed than the rest of the system, and outside the nodes – in unconnected areas – the speed may approach zero. There are thirty television sets for every thousand persons in sub-Saharan Africa, while the figure for North America is 796. More than half the Indian population has never made a telephone call, and while Internet coverage is well over 50 per cent in Europe, it is well below 1 per cent in most of Africa. In spite of a certain degree of deterritorialization, therefore, the central tenet of world-systems theory dividing the globe into centre, periphery and semiperiphery is still relevant in many respects.

Under a regime of accelerated change, obsolesence becomes an everyday thing. The anthropologist Andreas Huyssen (2003) relates a story of an attempt to buy a computer in New York, when he encountered unexpected difficulties: 'Whatever was on display was relentlessly described by the sales personnel as already obsolete, that is, museal, by comparison with the imminently expected and so much more powerful next product line' (Huyssen 2003: 70). Approaching parody, this anecdote nonetheless illustrates the incredible speed of change in certain domains, not least to do with consumption, communication and production. Commenting on accelerated consumption, Bauman writes:

> There is a natural resonance between the spectacular career of the 'now', brought about by time-compressing technology, and the logic of consumer-oriented economy. As far as the latter goes, the consumer's satisfaction ought to be *instant*, and this in a double sense. Obviously, consumed goods should satisfy immediately, requiring no learning of skills and no lengthy groundwork; but the satisfaction should also end – 'in no time', that is in the moment the time needed for their consumption is up. (Bauman 1998: 81)

We live in an era when the cigarette has replaced the pipe, cornflakes long ago replaced porridge (both the cigarette and cornflakes are now being replaced by nothing, which can be consumed even faster: increasingly, American children don't eat breakfast), e-mail is replacing paper-based correspondence, and the two-minute newsreel is one of the hottest products in the media field. The newspaper articles become shorter, the transitions in films more frequent, and the time each of us spends responding to an electronic letter is reduced proportionally to the number of e-mails we receive. The restless and shifting style of communication that was introduced with MTV has become an accurate image of the spirit of the age. Speed is an addictive drug: horrified, we watch ourselves groping for the fast-forward button in the cinema, the public loses interest in slow-moving sports; in my part of the world, ice skating and cross-country skiing have serious problems of recruitment and audience appeal as people switch to more explosive sports such as ice hockey and downhill skiing; we fill the slow gaps by talking in mobile phones when walking down a street or waiting for a traffic light to change; we damn the municipal transport authority when the tram is five minutes late, and consumers are still, after all these years, impatiently waiting for computers and Internet connections that are sufficiently fast.

With these examples in mind, we should not forget that accelerating technologies are extremely unevenly distributed. There are more telephones in Japan than in the 50 nations of Africa combined, Manhattan has more telephone lines than all of sub-Saharan Africa, and Italy has as many as Latin America.

3 ACCELERATION IN THE MEDIA

Journalism has always been a profession characterized by speed. The notion of today's paper is both a symbol and a sign of modernity. It is worth nothing if it is not *current*. Typically, the newspapers had their major breakthrough in the late eighteenth century, at the same time that clocks began to be used to monitor work; which was also the same period that the French and American revolutions introduced their individualistic freedom ideals and the Industrial Revolution began to transform labour. There was now a critical mass of people, especially in the major cities, who felt an acute need to keep up to date with contemporary events. Then, as now, a newspaper was ephemeral. Its lifespan lasted exactly one day.

Other media are faster. Radio and television can update their content at any time, and this is also the case with the media that will probably, within a few years, replace the newspapers, namely electronic publications based on text. (In this field, technological change happens so fast that there is little point in attempting to make accurate predictions, but it is worth noticing that a 'promising prototype' in 2006 had a passing similarity to book, but it was connected to the Internet and charged with 'electronic ink'.)

The Information Society

Acceleration hinges on technology, and the acceleration of global communication depends on information and communication technology. In fact, these technologies – from the cellphone to the computer terminal – are now so pervasive and so ubiquitous that many have taken to describing our era as an information society, or a 'global information society'.

Such terms are not unproblematic, and at the very least they need defining. Quite obviously, every human society is an information society in the sense that information is important for the distribution of social rank, for survival and so on. What distinguishes the contemporary era from previous ones is chiefly that information is rapidly becoming a central value generator for business and the most valuable raw material in the world economy (cf. Castells 1996). This is not just the case in the financial economy, or in that part of the economy that deals in information (such as software companies), but also in the industrial part of the economy.

In other words, the information society is not a 'post-industrial society'. Even in the most technologically advanced countries, such as Germany and the US, a large proportion of their economic output consists in industrial goods. What distinguishes the information society from industrial society is that in the former, electronic information technology pervades the productive process and is an important integral part of it.

It makes little sense to talk about the lifespan of an Internet newspaper: any item survives only until the staff has managed to update or replace it. The faster they are updated, the better is their reputation, the more hits they get, and more sponsorship. An average reader of the leading electronic newspaper in Norway – the only newspaper, incidentally, that does not have a paper version – spends 45 seconds browsing the paper. News addicts go there several times a day, especially during dramatic events (civil wars, hostage crises, football finals...). These kinds of media instil a new rhythm and a new restlessness, and – equally importantly – new routines in the consumption of news.

In a profoundly pessimistic and critical essay about the misery of television, Pierre Bourdieu (1996) develops a familiar, but far from unimportant argument. He claims that the fragmented temporality of television, with its swift transitions and fast-paced journalism, creates an intellectual public culture that favours a particular kind of participant. Bourdieu speaks of them as *fast-thinkers*. Whereas the Belgian cartoon hero Lucky Luke is famous for drawing his gun faster than his own shadow, fast-thinkers are described sarcastically as 'thinkers who think faster than an accelerating bullet'. They are the people who are able, in a couple of minutes of direct transmission, to explain what is wrong with the economic

The transition from an agrarian to an industrial society did not entail the end of agriculture, but its transformation. Agriculture was industrialized through new machinery and, to some extent, new forms of production and distribution. Similarly, the information society does not entail the end of neither agriculture nor industry, but their informatization. Sennett (1997) writes about a bakery in New England where the employees are no longer capable of baking bread, since the productive process is now managed via computer screens.

To take another, perhaps even more telling example: Before the so-called Y2K scare in late 1999, when it was widely feared that a huge number of mainframe computer systems would break down on 1 January 2000 because of simplified programming in the past, among the most anxious of all professional groups in the North were gardeners. The temperature in many greenhouses is regulated by thermostats run by computers. If the computers suddenly collapsed on New Year's Eve, enormous numbers of flowers would freeze across the cold part of the world. This is a way of describing the information society: it is a place where even the greenhouses have to be compatible with the latest operating system.

Needless to say, the informatization of the economy, and of society as such, takes place unevenly and chiefly in the rich countries and wealthy enclaves elsewhere.

policies of the EU, why one ought to read Kant's *Critique of Pure Reason* this summer, or explain the origins of early twentieth-century racist pseudoscience. It is nonetheless a fact that some of the sharpest minds need time to reflect and more time (much more, in some cases) to make an accurate, sufficiently nuanced statement on a particular issue. This kind of thinker becomes invisible and virtually deprived of influence, according to Bourdieu, in this rushed era. (In a banal sense, Bourdieu is obviously wrong. Few contemporary thinkers were, until his death in 2002, more influential than Bourdieu himself, and clearly he did not regard himself as a fast-thinker.)

Bourdieu's argument is congruent with the observation that media appeal has become the most important capital of politicians – not, in other words, their political message or cohesive vision. This is not an entirely new phenomenon; in the US, the first clear indication of this development came with John F. Kennedy's victory over Richard M. Nixon in 1960. Anyway, a result, in Bourdieu's view, is that the people who speak like machine-guns, in boldface and capital letters, who are given airplay and influence – not the slow and systematic ones.

What is wrong with this? Why should people who have the gift of being able to think fast and accurately, be stigmatized in this way? In a word, what is wrong about thinking fast? Nothing in particular, apart from the fact that some thoughts only function in a slow mode and that some lines of reasoning can only be developed in a continuous fashion, without the interruptions of an impatient journalist who wants to 'move on' (where?) in the programme. Bourdieu mentions an example that many academics will be able to identify with. In 1989, he published *La noblesse de l'Etat* (*The State Nobility*), a study of symbolic power and elite formation in the French education system. Bourdieu had been actively interested in the field for more than twenty years and the book had been long in the making. A journalist proposed a debate between Bourdieu and the president of the alumni organization of *les grandes écoles*; the latter would speak 'for' and Bourdieu would speak 'against'. 'And', he sums up sourly: 'he hadn't a clue as to why I refused.'

A topic Bourdieu does not treat explicitly, but which is an evident corollary of his views, is the diminishing returns of media participation following the information explosion. If, before the 1990s, one was invited to contribute to a radio or television programme, one appeared well prepared in the studio. One might shave (even if the medium was radio!), be certain to wear a freshly ironed shirt and a proper tie, and one went into the studio in a slightly nervous state determined to make one's points clearly and concisely. Nowadays, an increasing number of people in the know do not even bother to take part in radio or television transmissions and, if they do, their contributions frequently tend towards the half-hearted and lukewarm. As both viewers and guests on TV shows are aware, each programme has a diminishing impact as the number of channels grow, and the higher the number of channels and talk shows, the less impact does each of them exert. It is almost as if Andy Warhol was deliberately understating his point when, directly influenced by McLuhan, he said that in 'the future' everybody would be famous for fifteen minutes. (Today, he might have said seconds.)

In general, news is becoming shorter and shorter. A tired joke about the competition for attention among tabloids, consists in the remark that when war eventually breaks out for real, the papers will only have space for the 'W' on the front page. The joke illustrates the principle of diminishing returns (or falling marginal value). In basic economics courses, teachers tend to use food and drink as examples to explain this principle, which is invaluable in an accelerating culture: if you are thirsty, the first soda has very high value for you. The second one is also quite valuable, and you may even – if your thirst is very considerable – be willing to pay for the third one. But then, the many soda cans left in the shop suddenly have no value at all to you; you are unwilling to pay a penny for any of them. Tender steaks, further, are highly valuable if you are only allowed to savour them once a month; when steak becomes daily fare, its value decreases dramatically. The marginal value of a commodity is defined as the value of the last unit one is willing to spend money or time and attention on. Although this principle certainly cannot be applied to everything we do (a lot of activities, such as saxophone playing, become more rewarding the more one carries on), it can offer important insights into the situation Bourdieu describes – how news, and more generally information, is being produced and consumed. In this regard, it is easy to see that stronger effects are needed eventually, because the public becomes accustomed to speed and explosive forms of communication.

4 SIMULTANEITY

As the anthropologist Johannes Fabian (1983) has pointed out, there has always been a marked tendency in the West to think of peoples elsewhere as somehow belonging to another time. That which is distant in space is thought of as being distant in time as well. Even if the notion that 'primitive peoples' represented 'ourselves' at an earlier stage in social evolution was abandoned by professional anthropologists a hundred years ago, as a figure of thought this idea remained deeply embedded, even in anthropology itself, argued Fabian in the early 1980s. This kind of argument would have been difficult to sustain today.

There is a Gary Larson cartoon that depicts some unspecified tribal people shouting, at the imminent arrival of a group of people in khakis: 'Anthropologists! Anthropologists!' – whereupon they quickly put their TV sets and Playstations away, not to disappoint the researchers. Today, even in the places thought of as most remote from Western civilization, e-mail facilities are rarely far away and natives use cellphones if they can afford to. This does *not* mean that they are fully integrated into the 'flattened', globalized world described by the likes of Thomas Friedman – in many cases, they have no wagework, have never been to a large city, and continue to do most of their trade in the local market – but that they are hooked up to the world of instantaneous global communication. With both information technologies like television and communication technologies like e-mail and telephony becoming deterritorialized, there is a real sense in which humans everywhere have become contemporaries for the first time in history. Historical events such as the swift fall of Communism in Eastern Europe could be followed day to day by people everywhere (I was myself in Trinidad in the autumn of 1989, and had it been three years later, I could have discussed the events in Hungary

Popular music and temporal structures

In a bold and daring book about the qualities of progressive rock, the North American philosophy professor Bill Martin has tried, in his broad defence plea for rock groups he admires (including Yes, Rush and King Crimson), to explain what, to his mind, is wrong with the computer and studio based dance music developed since the late 1980s, including house, techno, drum'n'bass and other genres which have little in common, apart from the fact that they can be described as varieties of non-linear, repetitive, rhythmical dance music. This is music which in his view lacks progression and direction, which – unlike, say, Beethoven, Miles Davis and Led Zeppelin – is not heading anywhere. Enjoyment of such music is generally undertaken through entering a room full of sound where a great number of aural things are happening, and staying there until it no longer feels cool. Martin's preferred music is linear and has an inner development, although it may often be partly improvised. About the new rhythmic music, he has this to say:

As with postmodern architecture, the idea in this stacking is that, in principle, any sound can go with any other sound. Just as, however, even the most eclectic pastiche of a building must all the same have some sort of foundation that anchors it to the ground, vertically stacked music often depends on an insisting beat. There are layers of trance stacked on top of dance, often without much in the way of stylistic integration. (Martin 1998: 290)

Martin doubts that this music will be capable of creating anything really new. 'The vertical-stacking approach implicitly (or even explicitly) accepts the idea that music (or art more generally) is now simply a matter of trying out the combinations, filling out the grid.' There are layers upon layers on top of each other, every vacant spot is filled, and there is little by way of and Romania instantaneously with my North European friends by e-mail). People everywhere are exposed to certain versions of North Atlantic culture, and distance has become relative.

Still, it is important to keep in mind that not everything is in sync with everything else. Firstly, as Mittelman (2001: 7) points out, 'the [global] system affects its components in very different ways. Globalization is a partial, not a totalizing phenomenon. Countries and regions are tethered to some aspects of globalization, but sizeable pockets remain removed from it.' Hardly anywhere is this more true than in that aspect of globalization of which I speak as acceleration. Although there is an 'IT boom' in India, the country emerging as a major power in the production of information technology, more than half of the Indian population have never made a phone call.

---

internal integration. Stacking replaces internal development.

The listener's situation is radically different between rock/jazz and the new rhythmic music. The latter goes on and on; the former has a beginning, a long middle (internal development) and an end or climax. Interestingly, Indonesian gamelan music has been a significant source of inspiration to many of those who work with repetitive music, among them the minimalist composer Steve Reich. This is music developed in a traditional, ritualistic culture with no linear concept of development. The link with gamelan music is far from uninteresting, considering the view to the effect that an essentially non-linear way of being in time is being strengthened in contemporary culture.

Interestingly, Castells (1996) writes about new age music as the classical music of our era, and describes it as an expression for 'the double reference to moment and eternity; me and the universe, the self and the net'.

Desert winds and ocean waves create the backdrop for many of the repetitive patterns that make up new age music. It is a droning, timeless and lingering kind of music; an antidote to the quotidian rat-race, but also perfectly symmetrical to it as it brackets the passage of time.

Put differently: when growing amounts of information are distributed at growing speed, it becomes increasingly difficult to create narratives, orders, developmental sequences. The fragments threaten to become hegemonic. This has consequences for the ways we relate to both knowledge, work and lifestyle in a wide sense. Cause and effect, internal organic growth, maturity and experience; such categories are under heavy pressure in this situation. The examples from music are just illustrations. The phenomenon as such is more widespread, and both journalism, education, work, politics and domestic life, just to mention a few areas, are affected by vertical stacking, a result of acceleration.

Secondly, we all live in a number of different temporal regimes, the accelerated simultaneity of global information society being only one, and our participation in it varies from nil to considerable. Moreover, even the super-efficient, successful Indian computer engineer may occasionally visit a Hindu temple where time moves as slowly as it did a thousand years ago. Although there is a tendency for that which is fast to spread at the expense of everything that is slow (cf. Eriksen 2001a), slowness continues to exist both because of the exclusion of millions from the fast world of global capitalism and ICTs, and because significant sociocultural domains are scarcely influenced by it. Yet, for all the talk of acceleration and speed as markers of globalization, there have been few sustained studies of the variations in speed lived by people who are part of this.

5 SOME FURTHER IMPLICATIONS OF ACCELERATION

The sociologist John Urry (2000) has written usefully about the contrast between 'glacial' and 'instantaneous' time as two opposing temporal regimes, in a similar vein to what I have elsewhere (Eriksen 2001a) called cumulative, linear time and the time of the moment: 'Glacial' time is historical and developmental, whereas 'instantaneous' time is just now, with few connections with a past or a future. In a list of characteristics of instantaneous time, Urry mentions the technological changes dealt with above, a 'heightened temporariness of products, jobs, careers, natures, values and personal relationships', 'the growth of 24 hour trading', and 'extraordinary increases in the availability of products from different societies so that many styles and fashions can be consumed without having to wait to travel there' (Urry 2000: 129). All places now appear to be contemporary – but, as I have stressed before, we should pay more attention to the places that are not, and which are for obvious reasons rarely dealt with in studies of globalization.

Pessimistic analysts like Paul Virilio, who laments 'the pollution of distances and delays which make up the world of concrete experience' (Virilio 2000: 116), seem to overemphasize everything that is fleeting and transitory, and are fascinated with the extreme, at the expense of neglecting the mundane and everyday, where there may be more continuity. Yet, in spite of such objections, it is clear that global capitalism, both as a system of production, one of distribution and of consumption, favours speed over slowness because it is more profitable. As David Harvey sums up:

> Given the pressures to accelerate turnover time (and to overcome spatial barriers), the commodification of images of the most ephemeral sort would seem to be a godsend from the standpoint of capital accumulation, particularly

when other paths to relieve over-accumulation seems blocked. Ephemerality and instantaneous communicability over space then become virtues to be explored and appropriated by capitalists for their own purposes. (Harvey 1989: 288)

In this context, it is tempting to propose a whole series of contrasts that may illustrate the transition from industrial to informational society, from nation-building to globalization. We may, for example, depict the changes like this:

Industrial society	*Informational society*
CD/vinyl record	MP3
Book	WWW
Single-channel TV	Multi-channel TV
Letter	E-mail
Landline telephone	Mobile telephone

... and while we are at it, why not also:

Lifelong monogamy	Serial monogamy
The era of the gold watch	The era of flexible work
Ageing, maturing	Eternal youth
Depth	Breadth
Linear, cumulative time	Fragmented contemporariness
Scarcity of information	Scarcity of freedom from information

This list sums up some of the critical concerns voiced by many writers about acceleration and globalization. To what extent these contrasts accurately depict the contrast between two temporalities, one tied to the nation-state and industrialism, one tied to global networks and informationalism, is naturally subject to controversy, and this is not the place to give a final verdict. What should be noted is that all these assumed transitions point in the same direction, although the examples are taken from vastly different domains; the trend can be described as a movement from continuity and coherence (the book and the lifelong marriage as telling examples) to flickering fragmentation.

Every generation has a tendency to regard its own era as being unique, and with good reason: all epochs are in their way unique. At the same time, it can also be claimed that much of that which is perceived as novel, has in fact existed for quite a while – say, since Plato, or since the agricultural revolution, since Marco Polo, Columbus, Gutenberg, the Prophet Mohammed or the Reformation (take your choice). Regarding speed and acceleration, one may object, to those who stress the unique aspects of jet planes and the Internet, that the most important changes took place when the telegraph was invented, or the steamship, or for that matter the fast Roman two-wheel chariot. In other words, seen from this perspective, there is little or nothing new under the sun.

This kind of argument has its limitations. Although the telegraph was an invention with enormous consequences, the Internet signifies more than a mere footnote to Marconi. Global telecommunications based on real time create a framework for human existence that differs radically from all earlier technologies. Yet it is correct to regard the electronic revolution as a direct extension of earlier innovations and accelerations. The great informational divides in Western cultural history – writing, money, printing, the clock – contributed to liberating, as it were, communication from its immediate context; writing made knowledge timeless and cumulative, the clock made time mechanical and universal; money made values comparable. Whether one is in Canberra or in Kanpur, a dollar, an hour and a news headline mean pretty much the same. The circumstances continue to vary, but the common denominators link places together.

Standardization and time saving are true-born children of the Industrial Revolution, and it was during the disruptions caused by industrialization that the foundations for the tyranny of the moment were laid. Only in industrial society could the clock be used to promote syncronized efficiency in a large and complex industrial work setting. It was also in this era that time and money were tightly coupled; punctuality had been a virtue at least since the time of Erasmus, but the notion that time saved is money made became a guiding principle in production only when industry replaced traditional crafts on a large scale. The industrial revolution, which began towards the end of the eighteenth century, would need the entire nineteenth century to be completed in the West, culminating in the introduction of assembly lines and time recorders. The twentieth century ended with the globalization of simultaneity.

Chapter Summary

- Time-space compression refers to the 'squeezing together' of time and space due to economic and technological changes, and it appears as acceleration.
- Technologies that accelerate communication — from jetplanes to cellphones — have spread fast in the last decades, but unevenly, leading to the exclusion of vast numbers of humans, largely in the Third World.
- Both the logic of capitalist growth and expansion, and the availability of technologies of instantaneous communication, lead to acceleration in communication, production and consumption.
- A consequence of accelerated communication is the enhanced knowledge, even if skewed, of remote places in large parts of the world.

3 STANDARDIZATION

INTRODUCTION

Imagine a non-standard world. You would live in a town or village with your relatives, with few prospects of moving anywhere else. Everything you knew was handed down by your older relatives; all skills were taught face to face. The language you spoke was mutually intelligible with that of neighbouring areas, but not quite identical, and comprehension faded with distance. Trade with outsiders took place through barter, but within your local area certain goods could be exchanged for shell money. Your religion was associated with ancestors and the nature surrounding your home area. There was no script, no money, no calendars, no standards of measurement operating beyond the immediate neighbourhood.

In the pre-modern world, most products and services were non-standard. They conformed to no commonly established norm or set of parameters. They could not be mass produced, and if they travelled, they were recognized as exotic and precious. Language, too, was mostly local, spoken only in a restricted area and with marked dialect differences between localities. With the coming of literacy and later printing, the development of the modern state and its institutions (Anderson 1991 [1983], Gellner 1983), standardization of phenomena such as language, measurements and law took place at the national level. The development of the banking system contributed to the standardization of money and eventually other financial instruments.

In an important sense, globalization continues the work of nation building by creating shared standards, comparability and 'bridging principles' of translation between formerly discrete and sometimes incommensurable worlds (Barloewen 2003; Eriksen 2003; Meyer et al. 1992). Anything from consumer tastes to measurements and values is now being standardized at a global level. This does not mean that everybody is equally affected (it would be foolish to assume this), nor that standardization is perfect and all-encompassing. However, it is indisputable that the range of common denominators is widening in its scope and deepening in its impact, as a result of the accelerated disembedding processes discussed in the previous chapters.

I SOME STANDARDS OF A GLOBAL MODERNITY

Standardization implies comparability. Shared measurements ensure that a buyer in a distant land gets the amount he has paid for; shared temporality makes synchronization and timetables possible; a shared (or convertible) currency makes economic transactions across space easy; a shared language makes communication across borders possible. Some of the social and cultural features of modernity are preconditions for globalization – if rural Turks had not known about wagework they would not have migrated to Germany and if middle-class Brazilians had been illiterate, they could not have learnt English at school – and I will therefore run quickly through some of the most important forms of standardization entailed by modernity and required by globalization.

Firstly, a *monetary economy* has become the norm, if not a universal practice, in most parts of the world. Such an economy is encouraged by states, which receive important revenue through direct and indirect taxation. States have become the most powerful absentee landlords, and the omnipresence of money integrates an unlimited number of people anonymously into a vast system of exchange. The temporal structure on which this depends is linear and irreversible.

Secondly, *formal education* is nearly universally recognized as an important means for the achievement of rank, wealth and related benefits. This entails, among other things, literacy, the standardization of languages and the suppression of minority languages. Two hundred of the original 250 Australian languages have been eradicated, which is not only a testimony to literal genocide but also a strong indication of cultural genocide.

Thirdly, political units of significant importance to the majority of mankind are *political parties*, organized at a nation-state level with local branches. Position in political parties is ostensibly achieved, not ascribed.

Fourthly, official ideologies in virtually every country in the world are *nationalist* in character (although nationalism comes in many flavours) and individual rights and duties are to a great extent vested in their citizenship. For those who are deprived of citizenship – internally displaced people, certain minorities, certain asylum-seekers – it thus becomes very difficult to assert their rights. The nation-states require their citizens to adhere to an abstract ideology of metaphoric kinship and to make personal sacrifices for the betterment of the abstract community of the country. In return, the nation-state presumably offers protection, collective identity and career opportunities.

This list could have been made much longer, but I shall stop here. The main point is that the fact of the modern nation-state seems to create a uniform and universal framework for social organization on a very large scale. Of course, hardly any two persons are affected by these and other dimensions of modernity in the same way, but virtually everybody has to cope with aspects of the nation-state and capitalism. Hardly anybody is totally unaffected in the contemporary world.

2 SOME CONTEMPORARY FORMS OF STANDARDIZATION

Traditional craft skills were transferred directly from master to apprentice but production in a factory is so standardized that it ideally only requires a few, general skills. One of the aims of standardization of skills is to make workers interchangeable. As the early sociologists from Marx to Durkheim noted, production in a factory entails splitting up the process so that each worker only produces a tiny part of the whole. Criticism to the effect that this led to alienation was made not just by Marx, but by a lot of concerned observers in the nineteenth century – in other words a generation or two before Henry Ford invented the assembly line. Things would, in other words, only get worse. Or perhaps better: like books, manufactured goods became cheaper and more easily available as a result of mass-production and standardization.

Industrial production synchronizes work and standardizes its products. An item, such as say, an MP3 player, is identical with all other items of the same make and model and if it is unique that is because of some defect. In the society of craftmanship, on the contrary, each object was individually made and unique. Mass-produced objects are interchangeable, like workers' skills; they can be transferred to new contexts, and there are minimal problems of translation involved in adapting them there.

A world of standardization is a world of many common denominators and bridgeheads for communication.

Writing, money, wagework, the political party and the state are some of the key dimensions of standardization making global integration possible. The clock, mechanical time, is also important. The technology of the clock led to both the standardization of time units and the synchronization of large populations. The larger the number of people who needed to co-ordinate their movements with minute precision, the larger were the regions that were comprised by the new standards. When the last stretch of the Great Western Railway was opened in June 1841, the clocks in Bristol were ten minutes behind clocks in London. There had been no need for an exact synchronization of the inhabitants of the two cities yet. This need for synchronization came partly with the railway and partly with the telegraph during the following decades. The railway reduced the twenty-hour journey from London to Bristol to four hours, but the telegraph soon reduced the time required to send urgent despatches almost to zero.

The present global system of twenty-four time zones was established in 1884. A maze of local time zones had made conversion difficult earlier –train travellers had to set their watches in every city – and the need for a common standard had been voiced for years when an international panel finally reached an agreement at a meeting in Washington, DC.

Standardization is uneven. Speaking about the 'nodes' of global communication, such as airports, conference venues and business hotels, Ulf Hannerz (1990) proposes the term 'global switchboards'. Those who meet there, originating from different societies, speak a shared language (often English) and also have other things in common; they conform to a number of shared cultural standards. However, other members of their respective societies have less in common with each other, and are to that effect less standardized on a global scale.

EFL as the Medium of Globalbabble

Although the global percentage of native English-speakers is declining, the number of people using English as their main foreign language is growing. According to the British Council, about 25 per cent of the world's population speak English 'to some level of competence'; and they add, in a perhaps not overly disinterested vein, that 'demand from the other three-quarters is increasing.' 'Everybody wants to speak it' (http://www.britishcouncil.org/english/).

You may be reading this in a language different from the one you use as an everyday medium for carrying on with your life. As for myself, I'm writing in a language that is not the medium of my everyday trivia, and there are lots of things I cannot say in a satisfactory way through the idiom of English. Exactly how these limitations affect our communication is difficult to assess, but in general, English as a foreign language (EFL) has certain characteristics not shared

with English as a native language. In fact, there are courses available for translating between 'plain English' and EFL. One such online course, or really a teaser for a course (http://www.webpagecontent.com/arc_archive/139/5/), offers a great deal of advice — not, this time, for the foreigner wanting to express himself better in a foreign language, but for native speakers wanting to be understood by foreigners. As everybody knows, English as a foreign language is not the same language as English spoken by natives. More than one first-time foreign visitor to London, with top marks in English from his or her school, has been shocked upon discovering that it is plainly impossible to understand what the cockney cabman is saying.

The examples discussed in the online course are instructive in suggesting some changes to be expected when an increasing amount of communication takes

Standardization is attempted in many areas, and the goal is always to create comparability in order to enhance communication, trade and various forms of exchange. The plastic card and the bar code are two everyday examples of global standards that make interaction across boundaries easier. A much-publicized early twenty-first century attempt at standardization from a different field, moreover, is associated with the so-called Bologna agreement in Europe.

In 1999, ministers of education from twenty-nine European countries met to discuss the future of higher education in the continent. This was the starting point of a highly consequential and controversial restructuring of higher education in Europe, aiming to standardize courses and degrees continent wide, to enhance comparability, student mobility and to ensure consistent quality. As a result of the Bologna reforms, many countries have had to change their degree system dramatically, to conform to the requirements laid down for MA and BA degrees internationally. The advantages are obvious in that they create a 'level playing field' making it easy for students to

place between people who are not using their first language.

- One is advised to use short sentences.
- One is advised to avoid false subjects such as 'it' in sentences like 'It is extraordinary how warm the weather is'. It is better to say 'The weather is extraordinarily warm.'
- Miniwords, or fillers, such as get, go, lot, by, for, it, he, the, a, of, are discouraged as they can lead to confusion.
- Complex questions are discouraged, such as 'You don't have the courage to acknowledge that your allegations have no factual basis whatsoever, do you?' Rather say, 'Do you admit that you have made false allegations?' (I like this example. It prepares the native speaker for encounters he may expect with foreigners.)

- Similarly, double negatives are discouraged: 'The results were not displeasing' should be avoided. Instead say, 'The results were pleasing.'
- One is moreover advised not to use idioms such as 'the tip of the iceberg', 'just around the corner' and so on.
- Plainly, all kinds of ambiguity are discouraged to avoid misunderstandings. Negative words are also discouraged, as in 'The shipment will not arrive until late January' – it is better to say 'The shipment will arrive in late January.'

In other words, authors of courses like this one encourage native speakers to avoid colloquialisms and idioms, understatement and metaphor. The result can be described as a disembedded language, an efficient, simplified, practical means of communication where there would otherwise have been none.

take courses (or 'credit points') at various universities in different countries, and the standardized system of evaluation (using the Anglo-Saxon A-F scale) supposedly makes degrees from different universities comparable.

However, there are problems with such attempts at standardization. A grade on a BA course is not a metre; it has no objective standard to relate to. As a result, the grades are used differently in different countries (the grade A, I happen to know, is rarely given in Oslo). There are also serious misgivings about the assumed loss of local specificity and old academic traditions in several countries. The German Magister degree entailed years of independent study; it is now being replaced by a two-year taught MA degree. As is often the case, locals protest against standardization imposed from above or outside.

3 OBSOLESENCE

A consequence of standardization is that many practices, beliefs, skills and crafts disappear. The non-standard is either marginalized or rendered obsolescent, like beer bottles too tall to fit the standardized supermarket fridge shelves. This happens in many domains. A famous anthropological travelogue, Claude Lévi-Strauss's *Tristes Tropiques* (Lévi-Strauss 1989 [1955]), is largely built around the idea that entire life-worlds are being rendered obsolete by modernization. The onslaught of modernity, in Lévi-Strauss' view, entailed the loss of unique ways of life, world-views, real-life showcases of human variation as it were. A generation before Lévi-Strauss, the great Malinowski complained, a tad more cynically, that anthropology, or ethnology as he still called it,

> is in the sadly ludicrous, not to say tragic, position, that at the very moment when it begins to put its workshop in order, to forge its proper tools, to start ready for work on its appointed task, the material of its study melts away with hopeless rapidity. Just now, when the methods and aims of scientific field ethnology have taken shape, when men fully trained for the work have begun to travel into savage countries and study their inhabitants – these die away under our very eyes. (Malinowski 1984 [1922]: xv)

Nostalgic laments about the disappearance of unique cultural forms are a common feature of perceived globalization – indeed, a popular BBC series about other cultures was called *Disappearing Worlds*. This concern is not new – it is a part of modernity's critical self-reflection and can be traced at least back to the Romantic movement in Germany around the year 1800. However, the speed with which cultures (and other things) are rendered obsolete is greatly enhanced in our intensively globalized era. The quaint and local is replaced with that which is comparable along a set of common denominators in order to enhance intelligibility, trade, exchange and – many would emphasize – exploitation. General-purpose money of the Western type, thus, renders shell money and copper sticks obsolete; the great religions of conversion (Islam and Christianity) have conquered most of the societies that used to have local religions; formal education replaces learning by watching; and thousands of languages are predicted to vanish within a few decades. In the contemporary North Atlantic world, typical examples of obsolescence would refer to commodities such as locally manufactured soft drinks (in the early 2000s, it was reported that Coke was for the first time the largest-selling soft drink in Scotland, dethroning the national beverage Irn-Bru, which may eventually become obsolete) and computer operating systems (there were lots in the 1980s; now there are essentially three – Windows, MacOS and Linux).

A closer look at language obsolescence may be instructive in showing the forces of standardization and globalization at work. In a pre-standardized world, it was difficult to draw the boundary around one language. It was largely with printing and mass education that languages were standardized in the sense that a speaker from Bayern (Bavaria) could easily communicate with and relate to the same literary standard of German (*Hochdeutsch*) as a speaker from Schleswig.

Now, only a few of the world's several thousand languages underwent this process of standardization, which was often associated with the growth of a nation-state (Anderson 1991 [1983]). These languages often ousted or marginalized unwritten languages or even written languages with no political support. Nation-building, in this way, functioned as a great leveller.

In the early 2000s, the work of the nation-state continues, this time at a higher pace and on a larger scale. The linguist David Crystal (2000) estimates the number of languages spoken in 2000 as 6,000. Interestingly, only 4 per cent of these languages account for 96 per cent of the speakers. A quarter of them have fewer than 1000 speakers. Commonly, a language becomes obsolete when the speakers first become bilingual (adding a dominant language to their repertoire), followed by a decline in the use of their original language, largely for pragmatic reasons – the radio, the newspapers and the people in town all use the dominant language. It is widely believed that English is the main 'global leveller' here, imposing its standards on people everywhere else; so far, this is an overstatement. Bahasa Indonesia, the national language of Indonesia (which is almost identical to Malay) has probably eradicated more local languages than English. However, the growth of bilingualism in English has been phenomenal over the last few decades, and this is a process of globalization proper (neither imperialism nor nation-building) since most of the countries which adopt English as a second language today have no shared colonial history with Great Britain. Moreover, English as a second language is making inroads not chiefly among the small peoples speaking languages with no literature and no public sphere but among speakers of national languages like Dutch and Polish. Many specialists envision a future where English will gradually replace national languages in certain domains – in academic publishing, this has already largely happened – while the national languages, often in a hybridized form with many loanwords from English, continue to be used, at least for some time, in other fields. To mention but one example, there is great pressure on European universities now, especially in smallish countries like Portugal and Finland, to offer courses in English in order to facilitate student mobility. Thus we have entered a period of linguistic standardization that is not a result of nationalism or imperialism, but of transnational networking.

4 THE GLOBALIZATION OF NOTHING

In a very entertaining and creative book about standardization called *The Globalization of Nothing*, the sociologist George Ritzer (2004) contrasts what he sees as two pervasive tendencies in the contemporary world: the *grobalization* of nothing, and the *glocalization* of something. He defines glocalization as that which is 'locally conceived and controlled and rich in distinctive substance' (2004: 8), while grobalization is defined as 'generally centrally conceived, controlled, and comparatively devoid of distinctive substantive content' (2004: 3). In other words, standardized, mass-produced goods catering to an assumed common denominator of disembedded market tastes are the outcome of grobalization, while anything that couldn't have been produced anywhere but in a particular location is defined as glocalization.

Indirectly framing the debate about standardization, Ritzer says that there 'is a gulf between those who emphasize the increasing grobal influence of capitalistic, Americanized, and McDonaldized interests and those who see the world growing increasingly pluralistic and indeterminate' (Ritzer 2004: 80).

Concentrating largely on consumption, Ritzer distinguishes between the grobalization–glocalization of places, things, persons and services. The more personalized, placebound and unique something is, the more it is glocalized. For example, while a craft barn represents the glocalization of something, Disney World stands for the grobalization of nothing. A bar frequented because of its skilful bartender or because it is where one's friends hang out is 'something', whereas hotel bars with new customers every evening and a standardized, transnational selection of cocktails is a 'nothing'. The big and standardized stands for nothing whereas the small and locally fashioned stands for something in Ritzer's account.

Ritzer agrees that things are really more complicated. He admits that 'grobalization can, at times, involve something (for example, art exhibits that move among art galleries throughout the world, Italian exports of food like Parmigiano Reggiano and Culatella ham...)' (Ritzer 2004: 99), and conversely, that the glocal can also produce nothing, such as tourist trinkets. He even concedes that there are 'people today, perhaps a majority, who prefer nothing to something and who have good reason for that preference' (2004: 16), thinking about those – hundreds of millions – who scarcely have the opportunity to participate in the consumption of nothing. People in poorer countries produce much of the richer world's nothingness but can scarcely afford any of it for themselves.

Inspired by Marc Augé's concept *non-places*, but also by Max Weber's classic theory of disenchantment and rationalization, Ritzer establishes a series of simple contrasts where everything mass-produced, ready-made and instant appears dehumanized, and where everything which is one-of-a-kind (be it a product or an employee) is 'enchanted' and authentic.

Many writers on globalization would be inclined to see Ritzer's analysis as simplistic. As pointed out by Amselle (2001: 22), even in McDonald's restaurants, 'as one may discover by visiting its outlets throughout the world, [they] do not sell the same products everywhere'. In India, where the majority of the population does not eat beef, for example, the Big Mac is a lambburger. In addition, apparently identical products and services are *perceived* in distinctly local ways. Coca-Cola, an everyday product in most of the Western World, is associated with weddings and other rituals, for example among Luo of Western Kenya. The Macintosh computer, according to Amselle (2001), has become a symbol of identity among French intellectuals resisting the global dominance of Microsoft. In other words, rather than being overrun by the grobalization of nothing, locals invest the 'nothing' with something in discriminating, critical ways. And yet, Ritzer clearly has a point when he argues that the transnational standardization of commodities and services is one important dimension of globalization, even if the *meaning* of the products and services thus disseminated vary locally.

5 MCWORLD AND ITS DISCONTENTS

One influential writer on globalization who is likely to be sympathetic to Ritzer's perspective is the international relationist Benjamin Barber, whose book *Jihad vs McWorld* (Barber 1995) has exerted major influence inside and outside the academy – it is even rumoured that it was read by President Clinton. Thinking along similar lines to Ritzer, Barber is more interested in the *political* implications of globalization than its *commercial* ones.

Like Ritzer, Barber describes the emergence of a bipolar world pitting global capitalism and consumerism against local resistance and alternatives. The word 'jihad' in the title has led many to assume that Ritzer's book is somehow about the West and Islam, but he uses it as a generic term for all kinds of countermovements.

McWorld, in Barber's usage, 'is a product of popular culture driven by expansionist commerce'. It is a close relative to the old Marxist term 'monopoly capitalism' wedded to consumerism. Barber describes the spread of standardized popular culture, such as MTV, at some length, showing that nearly all countries outside Africa had access to MTV as early as 1995. This is relevant not only as a description of transnationally standardized consumption but also as an indicator of economic power. Comparing today's media magnates to earlier industrial tycoons, he reminds the reader that 'their is power not over oil, steel, and railroads – mere muscles of our modern industrial bodies – but over pictures, information and ideas – the very sinews of our postmodern world' (Barber 1995: 298). Although Barber shows how the oil oligarchy seems to stimulate local countermovements in many countries, among local people who are not beneficiaries of the giant corporations, he also seems to argue that standardized global media and information products lend themselves more easily to local political protest – they seem to be colonizing people's minds – than industrial products.

The Metric System

Britons, Americans and a few others have rebelled against it for decades, but the metric system is the closest bid we are likely to get for a universal, coherent global standard for all important measurements. Bushels, pounds, yards and ounces, and a myriad of locally defined measurement units across the globe, have been giving way to the metric system for two centuries, and the process seems to be nearly completed by the early twenty-first century.

Now officially named the International System of Units (SI), the metric system began in France in 1790, when a government commission defined the metre as one ten-millionth of a quarter of the earth's meridian passing through Paris.

At the first international General Conference on Weights and Measures in 1889, a prototype metre bar was established, made of 90 per cent platinum and 10 per cent iridium, measured at the melting point of ice. The metre is the standard from which all other units in the metric system derive. A litre (originally pinte) is defined as the volume of a cube having a side equal to a tenth of a metre (a decimetre). The unit for mass, the grave (now kilogramme), is defined as the mass of one litre of distilled water at the temperature of melting ice.

What is at stake for Barber, whose book is not just diagnostic but genuinely worried in its tone, is civil society and with it democracy. In a world where citizens can choose to either become integrated into a blandly homogeneous global market or to join an anti-modern resistance movement, he argues, there is little room for *the citizen* as a member of a public sphere deliberating over politics, making compromises and ensuring a fair distribution of goods and benefits. Like many others, Barber is not opposed to the market as such, but says that the virtues of the global marketplace 'scarcely warrant permitting the market to become sovereign over politics, culture, and civil society' (1995: 298). Barber's *jihad* metaphor resembles Ritzers notion of *the glocalization of something*, but it differs through its chiefly political content and for being overtly anti-global. Like all simplifications, Barber's dichotomous world can be criticized, but as a very general description of a global dynamics with manifold local expressions it stands up to scrutiny quite well. As a matter of fact, many if not most writers on the politics of globalization employ some kind of dichotomous divide between on the one hand, universalist globalizing processes and, on the other, local alternatives or resistance – 'cosmopolitans and locals' (Hannerz 1990), 'the Net and the Self' (Castells 1996), 'system world and

The decimal system on which the metric system is based is another globally accepted standard, a cultural one and not a god-given one. So is the Celsius system for measuring temperatures. Their almost universal acceptance (again, many Anglo-Saxons still swear by the Fahrenheit scale) is an instance of globalization, it has not come about by itself.

Even the A formats for paper (common almost everywhere ... except in some English-speaking countries) are based on the metric system. All formats are defined such that the height divided by the width of the paper is the square root of two. The rare format A0 has an area of one square metre. Format A1 is A0 cut into two equal pieces, and so on. This means that the common A4 format is one-sixteenth the size of A0, i.e $1/16$ m^2.

The metre as such is a fairly random unit, but all the other measurements of mass, density and so forth follow logically from it, and it is also used in compounds with other systems of measurements creating standards such as kilometres per hour.

life-world' (Beck 1999), 'fundamentalism and ambivalence' (Bauman 1998). These are simply attempts to give some substance to a general dichotomy between the universal and the particular.

6 MS WORD

There is a healthy and vigorous body literature dealing with standardization – some of it laudatory, some of it critical, some of it just curious – but surprisingly little is written about the medium of standardization through which more than 90 per cent of that literature is produced, namely Microsoft Word. This is even more surprising given that many critics of global homogenization through expanding markets are especially concerned about information technology and the media.

Microsoft Word, which began in the 1980s as one of many word processors on the market, gradually became market-dominant, and has virtually destroyed all competition in the world of Windows, where alternative word processors are difficult to come by. Most Macintosh users, too, use Word.

There is nothing remarkable about Word as a word processor, except for its size (it takes up an extraordinary amount of space on the hard drive). Its near-monopoly must be understood as a direct result of the dominant position of the associated operating system, Windows. Far from being a technologically innovative company, Microsoft has always imitated competitors and marketed its alternative more efficiently – Excel resembles Lotus, Word in its early incarnations resembled several Macintosh word processors (MacWrite, WriteNow and so forth), Explorer resembles Netscape Navigator, and the very Windows interface was in its day so similar to the Finder (the Macintosh's interface) that Apple sued for plagiarism.

Word is regularly launched in new versions, always larger and lumpier than their predecessors, often requiring the user to buy new hardware. Even if a user resists and wants to stick to his 1995 version of Word, he will eventually have to upgrade in order to be able to exchange documents with others.

How could it be that Word and Windows steadily increased their market shares from the early 1990s onwards, despite the existence of cheaper and (arguably) better alternatives? One answer, which gives an interesting spin on the discussion about standardization, is *path dependence* (David 1992). The more people who use a particular technological solution, the more difficult it becomes for an alternative to make headway, even if it is a better product. Nothing succeeds like success, and the dissemination of an emergent standard creates snowball effects, through deals with government agencies, major corporations and other big consumers.

The theory of path dependence has been criticized for not taking into account the possibility that consumers can change their minds. However, it should be said in defence of the theory that certain decisions are irreversible, and in a given network of communication and exchange, shared standards often enforce themselves. When a standard rail gauge (width of railway tracks) has been decided, there is no turning back afterwards. Nonetheless, the standards are not ubiquitous, and the standard gauge is used only by 60 per cent of the world's railways. Travellers by train from France to Spain, for example, have to change trains on the border because the tracks have different gauge. Several of the European countries that chose non-standard gauge did so for military reasons, to prevent alien powers from invading by train. This kind of argument is interesting in the context of the contemporary debate over how to prevent terrorists from entering one's country: the contrast shows how much more deterritorialized our present world is than that of the mid-nineteenth century.

Muslim countries and China have occasionally challenged the Christian calendar, generally without succeeding, while nobody, to my knowledge, has tried to posit alternatives to the colonially imposed global system of time zones. Microsoft's attempts to close the open standards on the Internet (through creating their own version of the HTML programming language) would, if it had been successful, create the same kind of path dependence as the clock and calendar standards: one could have stuck to the old, open source code, but in the end one would have few left to talk to.

This brings us to one of the clear advantages of standardization, seen from a user's perspective. Shared standards for time, measurements and word processing makes it easy to communicate across borders. It is easier to manage an organization where all employees use a single software package than one where people have chosen their software eclectically. Compatibility, support and networking are factors here.

Using MS Word can be a frustrating experience for writers who are accustomed to other word processors. It is difficult to turn its helper, spellchecks and automatic formatting off once and for all, and its menus are often counterintuitive. Fortunately, conversion filters are available for all non-standard word processors (that is to say, all except Word itself – the majority, as is well known, never has to learn the minority's language).

All word processors influence the way we write and think, by laying down incentives and constraints. For this reason, the historical transition from WordPerfect to Word as the dominant word processor is less trivial, from a cultural perspective, than the shifting market shares between say, Coke and Pepsi. The significance of Word's global dominance can be compared with the transition from parchment to paper, from the quill to the fountain pen: it influences language, the style of working and the style of thought. For this reason, an interest in software standards is not just motivated by an interest in standardization and globalization but it also has wider intellectual and moral implications.

7 HUMAN RIGHTS AND IDENTITY POLITICS

So far in this chapter, I have spoken of standardization in the domains of exchange (money), communication (language), political organization (the state) and a few aspects of everyday life (consumption). However, the flattening, or levelling, forces of standardization on a global canvas can be studied from other points of view as well. In fact, it may well be argued that the spread of human rights ideas and practices was one of the most spectacularly successful forms of globalization in the twentieth century.

First established as a global ethics when the embryonic United Nations passed the Universal Declaration of Human Rights in 1948, human rights are invoked frequently in politics at both the domestic, local and transnational level worldwide. A main critique of certain transnational business practices (see Klein 1998 for the standard reference here) has been their failure to respect the human rights of their workers. Debates about immigration into western Europe are often concerned either with human rights violations within immigrant groups (especially with respect to women) or with transgressions on the part of the majority. Powerful North Atlantic aid donors now use 'good governance', which includes the implementation of human rights, as a criterion for giving aid to poor countries. Rebel groups, petitioners and political minority groups worldwide use claims of human rights violations as their main claim to be heard.

The transnational monitoring of and canvassing for an extension of human rights has grown tremendously. NGOs, governments and UN agencies invoke human rights regularly. Specializations such as human rights and gender, or human rights and the environment, or human rights for indigenous groups, are firmly established in the global discourse about justice and ethics.

In its report on culture and globalization, *Our Creative Diversity*, the UNESCO (1995) simultaneously favours cultural diversity and the protection thereof and a global ethics based on a shared recognition of human rights. While the possible contradictions in this position have been pointed out (see, for example, Eriksen 2001c), the aim for the UNESCO (the United Nations Educational, Scientific and Cultural Organization) is to ensure the universal respect for some shared values, while simultaneously resisting global cultural homogenization. In other words, standardization at the level of morality is good in their view, but not at the level of expressive culture.

It has often been shown, not least by anthropologists, that human rights are always implemented in a particular local context (see Wilson 1997; Cowan, Dembour and Wilson 2001), meshing the universal with the particular in a 'glocal' way. Human rights have to be interpreted, contextualized and sometimes prioritized in order to be useful. Limitations on the use of the freedom of expression, for example, vary internationally. Whether to put the greatest emphasis on social and economic rights, for example, or civil and political rights, is a political issue. In some countries, governments make efforts to reduce income disparities and see this as a human rights question; in others, free competition (with ensuing disparities) is interpreted as conforming to human rights. In some societies, the freedom of the individual is seen as the highest value, while in others, the integrity of the family, which gives the individual security, is deemed more important.

Human rights are thus universal principles that, translated into practice, always have a local element. However, and this is important, they give most of the world a set of benchmarks, or a shared language of comparison, in which to frame their differences.

The notion of a *shared grammar* may be a very fruitful one when we consider various transnational flows and practices. Ethnicity, it could be said, is a means of rendering cultural differences comparable. There has evolved a global discourse about ethnicity that entails a great number of formal commonalities between ethnic groups struggling for recognition everywhere. The emphasis on cultural heritage, shared customs and a history of oppression is shared by ethnic minorities everywhere. To a great extent, they have learnt from each other, even if their battles are local and unique. We shall consider this in greater detail in the last chapter.

At a different level of identity politics, it could be argued that global communication makes it easier both to try to implement standardized forms of religion, and to resist such attempts. In a slower era, Islam would, from Morocco to Indonesia, appear in distinctly local forms without this posing a problem, Sunni Islam being a decentralized religion. In Morocco, saints were revered (like among the neighbouring Spanish Catholics); in Pakistan, the influence from Hinduism has been perceptible; in Indonesia, the articulation of Islam with *adat* (traditional custom) in its time led to the development of a local blend of Islam. With the increased mobility and instantaneous communication of the present age, the pressure to conform to certain standards is more perceptible than formerly. Puritan movements have arisen in Pakistan to purge Pakistani Islam of Hindu elements; and the *hijab* (headscarf), rare in Malaysia some decades ago, is now seen almost universally among Malay Muslim women.

8 THE NON-STANDARDIZED

Standardization, a key feature of modernity as such, is greatly facilitated on a transnational scale thanks to acceleration in communication, the predominance of a globalized capitalism, and the instruments of disembedding. It should nevertheless be kept in mind that the scope of global modernity, even if it is truly global, is not universal. In a strong critique of overenthusiastic 'globalizers', Jean-François Bayart (2003: 308) thus points out that 'the extension of capitalism to a world scale cannot be taken for granted.' He speaks of the 'ambiguous relationship to capitalism' in Latin America, sub-Saharan Africa's 'refusal to integrate into the capitalist economy' and the 'failure of 'political Islam' in defining a specific and viable economic orientation' (Bayart 2003: 309), concluding that globalization, certainly if we speak of it in terms of global capitalism, is patchy and far from comprehensive.

In other words, many languages may survive the twenty-first century – not because their speakers stubbornly stick to the idiom of their forebears, or because they are able to obtain support from transnational agencies favouring linguistic pluralism, but because they are left alone, overlooked, neglected by the globalizing forces. Research in this area must ultimately take on the question of whether this is a good or a bad thing. Isolated pockets of tribal people, say, in the New Guinea highlands, may avoid the oppression of the state, the disintegration of certain customs, the loss of language and oral traditions; but they will similarly not have the benefits of modern health care, a variety of job opportunities, a wider range of experiences and a more comprehensive freedom to shape their lives than before. What is to be preferred?

Regrettably, this kind of question is rarely relevant. The people Bayart has in mind are not, as a rule, isolated tribal people, but rather poor people in slums and impoverished peasants – uneducated people living in countries that accord them few citizen rights and marginal groups everywhere. However, he does not give a conclusive answer to the question of whether one is necessarily worse off for being marginal to world capitalism.

There can be no conclusive answer to this immensely important question, but in a very different part of the world, reflexive – that is to say, self-conscious – resistance to globalization has become widespread in certain milieus. It can be grouped in two main varieties. First, the so-called 'anti-globalization movement', a loose coalition of farmers, students and political idealists in the rich countries, have made strong protests and organized huge demonstrations against the instruments of global capitalism, particularly the World Trade Organization (WTO), arguing – among other things – that it is unfavourable to the needs of poor countries and that it leads to an unhealthy and demeaning standardization of production (notably agriculture) in the rich countries. It is to be noted here, and it has no bearing on the arguments put forward by the movement, that the 'anti-globalizers' are themselves globalized: they share a transnational mindset inspired by ideological developments in the North Atlantic, they communicate electronically and travel to demonstrations by jet. It is, in other words, globalization narrowly defined as global capitalism they rebel against.

A less visible, and less overtly political, form of political resistance to globalization is offered by the transnational 'slow' movements (see Honoré 2005), notably Slow Food and Slow Cities. Favouring traditional alternatives to the transnational and standardized (the 'nothing' in Ritzer's terminology), these movements emphasize the value of locally produced food and not least local food traditions, slowness as a value superior to speed in lifestyle questions, and a politics that puts 'the quality of life' before material standards of living. Typical Western middle-class phenomena, the 'slow' movements first emerged in northern Italy, where they are associated both with the preservation of medieval towns and with local specialties such as Culatella ham, wine and *lardo di Colonnata* (yes, it sounds like lard, and lard it is – cf. Leitch 2003). In Ritzer's scheme, the slow movements fit the category of 'the glocalization of something' since they play by the rules of global capitalism but try to fill it with something local and untranslateable.

Exclusion is a major theme in research on globalization and it affects many more people than those participating in either anti-globalization or the slow movements. For many of the millions of poor in the Third World, who have only experienced the negative effects of globalization (such as loss of land, pauperization, loss of tradition and autonomy), being 'standardized' to the extent of getting an education and a job at the local McDonald's would in many cases be preferred to being neglected. Capitalism creates both wealth and poverty simultaneously in the lack of a state, or a transnational political body, serving the needs not only of the market but of society. This gap – between a globally standardized and synchronized economic system on the one hand, and weak transnational political instruments on the other – can probably be described as the main contradiction, or source of conflict, in a globalized era. Some want the train of globalization to stop so that they can get off; others want it to stop so that they can get on. But both groups depend on a political power willing and able to create conditions for a society that contains more than standardized market forces.

Chapter Summary

- Standardization refers to the imposition of shared standards which render events and objects comparable and 'conversion' or 'translation' possible.
- Standardization entails the establishment of common denominators, but it also marginalizes and sometimes destroys that which is locally unique.
- In some cases, as with language, global or international standards coexist, through a stable division of labour, side by side with the local.
- Many of the tensions and conflicts resulting from globalization are based on a contrast between universalizing standardization and local alternatives or resistance.

4 INTERCONNECTEDNESS

INTRODUCTION

A sensible rule of thumb for connectedness might be that the actions of powerholders in one region of a network rapidly (say within a year) and visibly (say in changes actually reported by nearby observers) affect the welfare of at least a significant minority (say a tenth) of the population in another region of the network. Such a criterion indubitably makes our own world a single system; even in the absence of worldwide flows of capital, communications, and manufactured goods, shipments of grain and arms from region to region would suffice to establish the minimum connections. (Tilly 1984: 62)

The culinary capital of India may be London, that of China San Francisco. In order to carry out anthropological fieldwork in a village in the Dominican Republic, one has to spend at least a few months in New York City. The little trolls, 'Scream' t-shirts and expensive knitted sweaters sold to tourists visiting Oslo, are made in Taiwan, Pakistan and Sri Lanka, respectively. The largest city in the English-speaking Caribbean is London. And if the classical patriarchal kinship system of the Taiwanese had been unable to withstand the pressure of individualism from modernization, several shop owners in Silicon Valley might still have been in business: The patriclan is an efficient economic unit where interest-free loans and free services are available, and when shops in California (and elsewhere) have to close down because their customers have lost their jobs, this is partly a result of competition from East Asia.

Such is the extent of global interconnectedness – and I still haven't even mentioned satellite television, the Internet, cheap flights and cellphones. Some theorists compare the complex webs of connectedness in the current era to chaos and complexity in physics (for example, Thrift 1999; Urry 2003), mining complexity theory for models that can be used to understand social change.

The most famous image from chaos theory is that of the butterfly effect: A butterfly flapping its little wings on the Brazilian coast whips up some air and changes the direction of a tiny wind. This wind connects to other streams of air, changing parameters in the atmosphere ever so slightly for each step, and one of the cumulative effects is, say, a blizzard in Maine. The reasoning behind the butterfly effect is old as the hills, as witnessed by this familiar English rhyme:

> For want of a nail, the shoe was lost;
> For want of the shoe, the horse was lost;
> For want of the horse, the rider was lost;
> For want of the rider, the battle was lost;
> For want of the battle, the kingdom was lost;
> And all from the want of a horseshoe nail.

The general point here is that small changes can have momentous effects, or rather, that tiny variations in the initial parameters of a process may, through complex feedback processes, may lead to major differences in the outcome. Now, 'butterfly effects' as such are rarely observed in globalization processes, but the point is rather that in a steadily more interconnected world, the distance between cause and effect is often enormous. Space is relativized; urban Trinidadians may feel that Barbados and even Miami are closer than Mayaro in rural Trinidad, and although you exercise little power over your neighbour, you may work in a company with the power to hire and fire people in a Malaysian town. In this kind of world, the power of the nation-state is increasingly questioned. While few contend that the state is 'withering away', its power to govern is being challenged from several directions, all of them transnational – large corporations, transnational rights movements or religious ones, and ultimately the world market. Global climate change and other environmental issues demonstrate well that single states are unable, on their own, to regulate the conditions for their own survival. Media flows, flows of people, of goods and of commitments, virtual communities on the Internet and transnational interest groups undermine the power of the nation-state to some extent. The question, and here scholars disagree, is to *what* extent.

Few would disagree that the boundaries between societies and cultures, which were never absolute, are becoming increasingly contested. Charles Tilly's pioneering book *Big Structures, Large Processes, Huge Comparisons* (Tilly 1984) argued that social science and sociology in particular ought to develop a truly global outlook, leaving the 'pernicious postulates' of classic sociology behind, which presupposed that the world as a whole can be divided into distinct societies, that social change is a coherent general phenomenon, that large-scale change takes all societies through a more-or-less standard set of stages, and that times of rapid change necessarily entail a range of disorderly behaviours such as crime, suicide, and rebellion. In contemporary language, one might say that Tilly calls for a transnational, non-teleological social science able to hold its own when confronted with paradoxical complexities.

First, it is clearly not the case that the world is 'moving in one direction', nor that modernity entails the death of everything non-modern. Kinship continues to play an important role even in the most modern and individualist societies in the world; religion continues to be important, both as personal religiosity and as organized religion; and interpersonal trust and informal networks continue to function as a crucial 'glue' even in thoroughly bureaucratixed societies.

Second, 'methodological nationalism', to use Beck's more recent (2000) term, in Tilly's view seriously limits the comparative scope and contextual understanding of sociology. It is plainly impossible to understand a single nation-state, even a huge one, if the analysis is not based on an understanding of transnational processes. Transnationalism must be a premise, not an afterthought.

Many sociologists and other social and cultural theorists have, in the decades following Tilly's book, taken his admonitions seriously – in addition to those, such as Immanuel Wallerstein (1974–9) and Eric Wolf (1982), who were already working within a global framework. One of the most comprehensive recent attempts to define and delineate a sociology of globalization is arguably Manuel Castells' three-volume *The Information Society* (Castells 1996–8; updated editions have been published later). The central idea in Castells' fifteen-hundred pages work is that of interconnectedness, and he approaches the issue from numerous viewpoints in a bid to show that the emergent world of transnational informational capitalism is qualitatively different from the one that preceded it.

I THE NETWORK SOCIETY

The central concept in Castells' first volume (Castells 1996) is the network, which in his view 'constitute the new social morphology of our societies' (1996: 469). What he argues is that the main mode of social organization in politics, the economy and civil society is shifting from the relatively stable hierarchy to a more fluid network form. The networks are interpersonal, transnational and transitory. Although a fixed hierarchy is absent, networks do not accord equal power to all. While the most powerful person in a hierarchy could be located to the top of a pyramid, the most powerful person in a network is the spider, the one to whom everybody has to relate, who knows everybody and can coordinate activities. In other words, the greatest personal capital in a network society belongs to the best connected person.

According to Castells, 'our societies are increasingly structured around a bipolar opposition between the Net and the Self' (1996: 3). In this he means that the main conflicts take place between autonomy and dependence, the life-world and the system-world (Niklas Luhmann's terms) or, put more prosaically, between 'abstract, universal instrumentalism, and historically rooted, particularistic identities.' Networks are not necessarily transnational, but this is increasingly the case, finds Castells, who sees the deregulation of world markets, the growth of information technology and the end of the Cold War as parallel processes creating conditions for an accelerated and intensified globalization.

Put differently, the concept of 'the Net' combines two related processes, namely economic globalization and the spread of information technology that makes distance irrelevant. Whereas classic industrial society was organized through 'the space of places', information society takes place through 'the space of flows', where the degree of connectedness, not physical proximity, is the decisive factor.

Networks are built around nodes, that is points where lines intersect or, less technically, a site where relevant activities connected with other activities (or nodes) elsewhere take place. A node can be and often is a person with relevant connections to others. Networks are, importantly, 'open structures, able to expand without limits, integrating new nodes as long as they are able to communicate within the network' (Castells 1996: 469).

Let us take a brief look at some of the transnational networks that contribute to making the world a smaller place.

2 COMMUNICATION NETWORKS

Communication networks are obviously of prime importance, nobody denies this, not even the 'globalsceptics'. The Internet, which was invented under the name Arpanet in 1969, had few and specialized users for two decades. Between 1995 and 2005, the number of people who had access to the Internet grew from 26 million to over a billion (http://www.internetworldstats.com). The number of Web sites worldwide has grown from nil in 1992 (the year the WWW was introduced) to a hundred million in 2000 and 450 million in 2006 (www.isc.org).

Mobile telephones were rare as late as 1990, which was before most countries had a telecommunication infrastructure ensuring coverage. Many 'mobile phones' were then just carphones jacked into the lighter socket of the car and connected with a huge transmitter/receiver in the boot. By 2006, the global number of mobile telephones is approaching the 2.6 billion mark, up from ten million in 1991. In China alone, 400 million people had a mobile phone in 2006, and they sent almost half a billion text messages every day.

Although networking through computers and mobile phones is in principle spaceless and deterritorialized, most of it is local. The most popular Web sites are usually, if not always, domestic ones, and the vast majority of SMSs sent have a local adressee. Still, both technologies bear the mark of the network. On my first field-work in Mauritius, in 1986, making a phone call home was exhausting, expensive and unsatisfying. In the late 1990s, I could comfortably speak to anyone from a terrace overlooking the Indian Ocean, far from the nearest town. Both e-mail and mobile phone calls militate against firm hierarchies: they are 'flat', immediate media of communication with no intermediate secretary or other filter between the sender and the receiver. Formal modes of address are unusual in both media – polite forms of address are in fact disappearing in several languages, possibly partly as a result of the new media – and communication through e-mail or cellphone is expected to be swift and efficient.

Much of the communication is in fact transnational. The number of transatlantic voice paths grew from 100,000 in 1986 to more than 1.9 million a decade later. The figures for transpacific voice paths are 41,000 in 1986 and 1.1 million in 1996 (Held et al. 1999: 343).

Still not satisfied that the global network society is a fact? Well, take the communications satellite. These satellites are used for a number of purposes, from weather forecasting to telephony, surveillance, television transmissions and, more recently, GPS navigation – you can now buy a box, place it on your dashboard, plot in your itinerary, and a pleasant voice will tell you exactly where to turn right and where to turn back (the only snag is that she has no information on traffic jams yet).

The communications satellite was first described by the science fiction writer Arthur C. Clarke in a short article published in 1945. It took nearly twenty years before the first successful experiments were conducted with communication satellites – parts of the 1964 Tokyo Olympics were televised via satellite – and in 1965 there was one such satellite. By 2006, there are more than 200, in addition to all the other, specialized satellites used for scientific research and other purposes. In the mid-1960s, a few million watched television programmes broadcast via satellite; today, several billion do. In principle, anyone can watch any programme although in practice, most people watch local programmes anyway.

Well over half the global population is to some extent affected by the tele-communications revolution, but to many it makes little subjective difference in their everyday lives. Contrary to the expectations of many, the Internet and mobile telephone are mostly used locally or domestically. Sometimes it seems that it was easier for a north European to get a penfriend in Brazil back in the 1970s than it is to join a virtual chatroom today. Nonetheless, the placeless character of the new technologies affect all who use them, even if unconsciously. A standard opener for a contemporary telephone conversation is, 'Where are you now?' This would not have been the case in the era of landlines, which predominated in most of the world until the mid-1990s.

Transnational media, drawing on the same satellite technology as the new communication technologies, lead to similar forms of deterritorialization, but it would be difficult to argue that the transnationalization of media lead to global homogenization. Rather, as many writers in the field have shown (see, for example, Hannerz 1996; Hemer and Tufte 2005), what is being globalized are chiefly the media *forms* not the content. National public spheres are to some extent being deterritorialized, when you can access your daily newspaper on the Web from anywhere in the world or watch your favourite domestic sitcom every Wednesday on your travels, but such examples testify to the enduring strength, not the dissolution, of national public spheres. Content on the Internet is often believed to be largely in English; in fact, only about half of it is. There are thousands upon thousands of Czech, Japanese, Spanish and Danish websites in existence. They share the technological form of the Web and its deterritorialized character, but not necessarily anything more.

3 A NETWORKED GLOBAL ECONOMY?

Castells, among others, writes about 'the network enterprise' as a new kind of company. It is loosely organized, there is little job security, it has assets in several places and it stands in a complex relationship to other businesses. Many have described recent changes in capitalism as a transition from mass production to flexible production (and accumulation), or from Fordism to post-Fordism. This means a shift from large, stable enterprises, often involving assembly lines and mechanized production of large quantities of standardized goods. With the growth of a diverse world market and rapid technological changes, this system became too rigid and was to a great extent replaced with a more flexible system of production, which was more responsive to market trends and more adaptable. Another trend described by Castells (1996) is the 'crisis of the large organization'; much of contemporary job creation and innovation comes from middle-sized and small enterprises functioning in a larger network of complementary and competing businesses.

On the other hand, some huge corporations have grown and benefited from increased globalization, adapting to the new situation. By 2004, Unilever had more than 500 subsidiaries located in 100 countries; and the mass media conglomerate Bertelsmann had more than 600 affiliates in 50 countries (Scholte 2005: 178). Production sites are more easily moved overseas than ever before, and markets are more easily accessible than they used to be. Certain services can easily be outsourced overseas, American call centres in India being the most commonly cited example (but if you call Norwegian Airlines' service number, the person taking your call would be an Estonian addressing you in flawless Norwegian). Statistics confirm the feeling shared by many to the effect that transnational corporations are becoming ever more powerful. Some of them have a turnover which exceeds the GDP of many countries, and the annual total sales by all companies which form part of transnational corportions increased from $2.7 trillion in 1982 to $17.6 trillion in 2003 (Scholte 2005: 179). Many of these companies are believed to be locally owned and run, and many are joint ventures with local capital; the point is that these figures suggest a tighter integration and closer networking in the global economy than earlier.

Tellingly, the very technologies that make networking possible have moved to the core of the global economy. Some of the fastest growing companies in the world deliver hardware, software or services associated with computing. Nokia, which basically produced rubber boots and a few TV sets in the 1980s, now sells more than 300 million mobile phones a year. Both IT companies, some telecommunications service providers (like Vodafone) and content producers like Time Warner, Bertelsmann and Sony are now among the most profitable corporations in the world.

The now virtually universal existence of capitalism as a system of production, distribution and consumption on the planet – the monetary economy, supply-and-demand mechanism and wagework are present almost everywhere – is underpinned by the breadth of economic involvement by major enterprises. The network structure of the global economy – with subsidiaries, joint ventures, a global scattering of assets – have led critics like Antonio Negri and Michael Hardt to describe the new world in bleak terms. Hardt and Negri, in their much-discussed book *Empire* (2000), depict the world as being ruled by a web of overlapping networks of transnational corporations and organizations – an empire with no geographical centre and without a government or an executive committee. Their vision is like a dark version of Castells' account of the network society.

Not everyone agrees that the world economy has entered a distinctly global phase. Hirst and Thompson (1999) are among the most vocal critics of the globalizers' views. They argue that:

- in some respects, the contemporary international economy is less integrated and open than that of the period from 1870 to the First World War;
- most ostensibly transnational companies are in fact based and firmly rooted in national economies;
- most investments take place domestically or among the rich countries, and
- the major economic powers (Europe, North America, Japan) are able to regulate and control important aspects of the world economy if they coordinate their policies.

Hardt and Negri appear to exaggerate the reach of the global network society (and so, probably, does Castells). Governments still regulate domestic trade and use incentives at home, often with tangible results. Environmental problems, usually blamed on globalization, are often the result of government policies, such as the Brazilian government subsidies to logging companies (Gilpin 2002). There is nothing even resembling a global labour market, given the severe restrictions on immigration in rich countries. As a citizen, you are endowed with particular rights and obligations towards a territorial state, and some states continue to maintain ambitious welfare programmes for all their citizens. As the ex-World Bank executive Joseph Stiglitz quips, in a bitter critique of the free-trade hypocrisy he has seen in international organizations, the Americans are all for free trade, but against imports (Stiglitz 2002). In other words, there are few reasons to believe that the global network society is omnipresent and omnipotent. Yet, a look at the figures is sufficient to convince me, at least, that there are strong tendencies towards wider and denser transnational networks, which lead to new forms of capital accumulation and increased concentration of economic power. Interestingly, the patterns of capital accumulation largely follow the centre-periphery-semiperiphery triad developed by Wallerstein, although the rise of East Asia as contender for a place in the centre is a new development. Countries like Brazil, South Africa and Russia remain semiperipheral, and Western Europe and North America (plus Japan and Australia) remain part of the centre.

Networks do not preclude centralization. Writing about transnational business, Sassen points towards the emergence of an 'inter-urban geography that joins major international financial and business centres: New York, London, Tokyo, Paris, Frankfurt, Zurich, Amsterdam, Los Angeles, Sydney, Hong Kong', more recently incorporating cities like São Paolo, Buenos Aires, Bombay, Bangkok and so on (Sassen 2003: 271). The point is that as these intercity networks have become denser because of the growth in transnational financial transactions, the distance between the cities and other parts of their countries has increased. Networks are open-ended, but their boundaries can be as rigid as those of the closed structure.

4 GLOBAL GOVERNANCE?

What about politics? Many writers on globalization have pointed out that the degree of transnational economic connectedness far exceeds the degree of transnational political regulation. As Held and McGrew (2000: 26-27) put it, 'the globalization of economic activity exceeds the regulatory reach of national governments while, at the same time, existing multilateral institutions of global economic governance have limited authority because states, jealously guarding their national sovereignty, refuse to cede them substantial power.'

It should nevertheless be borne in mind, as Held and McGrew also point out (2000: 11-12, see also Held et al. 1999: 54), that the number of international organizations has grown enormously in the last hundred years. The number of international NGOs (non-governmental organizations) was 37 in 1909, and had grown to 47,098 in 2000. The 'degree of diplomatic connectedness' between states, defined as the number of connections through at least one resident emissary, grew from 2,140 in 1950 to 5,388 in 1970 and 7,762 in 1991.

International co-operation has, in other words, grown tremendously in recent decades. Much of it falls short of deserving the label 'global', being only international: development co-operation and diplomatic ties, which account for much of the growth, tend to be bilateral and governed by nation-states. Truly transnational organizations are more interesting, and they proliferate in areas such as environmentalism and human rights issues. Such non-state, often network-based organizations may exert considerable political influence. Nevertheless, when one speaks of *global governance*, one usually has something more in mind, something that is binding on states and commits their power to a transnational good. International treaties concerning, say, workers' rights or greenhouse gases, are attempts at global governance, of an admittedly limited scope. International peacekeeping forces also express, from a different area, an ability among a number of countries to give up, temporarily, some of their sovereignty and use their diplomatic and military power to help resolve conflicts in which their country has no direct interest.

As a counterpoint to Negri and Hardt's grim outlook, George Monbiot (2003) has suggested the establishment of a world government, building on and extending both the power and the democratic legitimacy of the United Nations' General Assembly. Seen by many as utopian, this kind of proposal illustrates the widespread feeling that everything seems to be globalized except democracy. Summing up some of the main obstacles to global governance, Fred Halliday concludes that:

> the success of peace-keeping ... continues to run up against the reluctance of sovereign states to commit their forces to combat, and of states criticized by the international community to yield to UN pressure; growing awareness of the ecological crisis ... goes together with contention and evasion, in north and south; the rising recognition of the importance of women's position in society has produced outright rejection of change in some states, in the name of sovereignty and national tradition...; a greater stress on the rights of individuals produces denunciation of international, and specifically 'western', interference from others. (Halliday 2000: 498)

An additional argument against the idea of global governance is the idea that its instruments 'are not and are not likely to be democratic' (Dahl 2000: 538) because they may lead to majorities consistently overruling minorities. Against this pessimism, David Held (2005) has forcefully put the case for a cosmopolitan social democracy aiming to extend rights and obligations globally and to prevent meaningless wars. The discussion about the prospects and limits for global governance is bound to continue for some years – indeed as long as the gap between economic and communicational integration and political nationalism remains.

An alternative perspective sees the increased contact across borders as a source of conflict due to competition over scarce resources, deep cultural differences and the loss of ideological differences due to the end of the Cold War. The most influential representative of this school of thought is Samuel Huntington (1996), a political scientist famous for his notion of 'the clash of civilizations'. In Huntington's view, the most important conflicts in the world of the near future are likely to follow 'civilizational faultlines' – that is, they will be fought across the border areas between 'civilizations'. In Huntington's view, a civilization is a cluster of closely related cultures which forms 'natural' alliances. There is a 'Western' civilization, a 'Latin American' one, an 'Islamic' one, a 'Hindu' one and so on. However, so far, few conflicts in the world have followed the lines predicted by Huntington (Fox 1999), and his concept of the civilization has been criticized for being simplistic and based on an obsolete idea of the world as consisting of clearly bounded, territorial cultures.

Anarchist Connectivity in Early Globalization

Benedict Anderson, best known for his influential book on the growth on nationalism, *Imagined Communities* (Anderson 1991 [1983]), has more recently published a book about 'anarchism and the post-colonial imagination', which he describes as an essay on 'early globalization' (Anderson 2005).

Set in the Philippines of the late nineteenth century, Anderson's book describes the growth and indeed the invention of the Filipino nation, focusing on the role of a handful of intellectuals – the novelist José Rizal, the folklorist and journalist Isabelo de los Reyes, the political leader Mariano Ponce and a few others.

This was the era of the steamship and the intercontinental telegraph, a period that must have appeared dizzyingly novel, with fast communications and a shrunken planet. Anderson describes how the Filipino intellectuals were crucially influenced by events elsewhere in the world and how their personal networks covered most of the planet. Taking courage from the insurgencies of Cuba (another Spanish colony), Filipinos rebelled unsuccessfully against Spanish rule; they learnt from anarchists in France, syndicalists in Spain, humanist scholars in Germany, nationalists in China and modernizers in Japan. They were cosmopolitan in their outlook and transnational in their networks.

An obvious question that can be raised in connection with Anderson's book, is 'What has changed? In what important ways is our period of globalization and

5 TRANSLATION

The global dominance of English is reflected in many ways, not least through the linguistic insularity, indeed parochialism, of the English-speaking parts of the world. On a wonderful Web site called 'Index Translationum' (http://portal.unesco.org/culture/en/), UNESCO has collected a variety of statistical material on translations between 1979 and 2002. It reveals that 834,856 books were translated from English in that period – the figures for French, the runner-up language, are 141,801, and for Finnish 5,888.

Regarding target languages, the German-speaking world is the keenest on being enriched by writing from abroad: 243,144 books were translated into German (only 141,129 books were translated from German), whereas 164,794 books were translated into English. An impressive 36,898 books were translated into Finnish.

In other words, while the Finns translated more than six times as many books as the number of Finnish books published abroad, and the Germans translated nearly twice as many into German as were translated in the opposite direction, more than five times as many books were translated from English as into English. While just 5.4 per cent of the books translated from German in 2002 had English as their destination language, more than two-thirds of the books translated into German were from English.

---

transnationalism distinctive and different from the late nineteenth century, which was also a period of powerful nationalist ideology, capitalist expansion and technological innovations?'

One striking difference is to do with language. The Filipino intellectuals described by Anderson corresponded in many languages, since – as the author puts it – there was no 'ugly, commercially debased "international language"' available at the time. Another difference is to do with speed – travel from the Far East to Europe still took weeks. A third difference is that capitalism, while already hegemonic, was far less widespread then than it is now. Yet, at the same time, many of the social and cultural dimensions we associate with globalization today were already in place, in embryonic form, then – and this is Anderson's point. French ideas could be borrowed to be transplanted instantly to East Asia, local ways of life could be compared with those elsewhere through a growing scholarly literature, and a global consciousness about political change and human rights was spreading in Europe and the colonies. There was disembedding, movement, interconnectedness, acceleration and mixing – not to the same degree as now, but Anderson's book is still a reminder that contemporary globalization has been under way for quite some time, and that it may well be seen as an integral aspect of modernity as such.

It is quite difficult to believe it, but if the UNESCO statistics are correct, more books were translated in Denmark (5 million inhabitants) than in the United States (300 million inhabitants); and more books were translated in poor Bulgaria than in the rich United Kingdom.

According to statistics on Internet use, 51.3 per cent of communication on the Internet is in English (although a mere 5 per cent of the world's population speaks it as their first language). Regarding academic publishing, I have been unable to find reliable figures, but everyone seems to agree that the proportion of English has increased steadily since the Second World War. In some fields, more than 90 per cent of publications are in English.

6 REMITTANCES AND CHEAP CALLS

Contemporary migration is arguably better described as the ongoing negotiation of transnational ties than as a one-way movement creating permanent diasporic populations in host countries – to be integrated and eventually assimilated after one, two or three generations. Migration will be dealt with in some detail in the next chapter; for now, one dimension of migration will suffice to demonstrate some of the many emergent forms of interconnectedness criss-crossing the world, namely remittances.

Remittances are transfers of money from migrants to relatives or other close associates in the home country. In the USA, a main immigrant country, the value of remittances sent from the country is estimated to have grown from £2.15 billion in 1981 to £13.4 billion in 2003 – a sixfold increase in slightly over twenty years (Congress of the United States 2005). The remittances from the US were significantly larger than the total value of official American development aid.

Globally, the total amount of *formal* remittances increased from slightly over £1 billion in 1970 to £55 billion in 1999. However, the *informal* remittances transferred outside the banking system are estimated to be twice or three times the formal ones, which means that the total value of remittances from migrants in 1999 can have been as high as £150 billion (International Labour Organization). The value of remittances may thus exceed that of global foreign aid.

There is, in short, a massive transfer of wealth going on from the rich countries to the poor ones, which takes place at an individual, small-scale level and is therefore relatively unknown outside policy and research circles, and which shows the extent of interconnectedness between migrants and the people they have left. A precondition for remittances to function efficiently is trust and moral obligation, which continue to be operative years and decades after the migrant's departure. With informal transfers, this is even more the case than with formal money transfers: very often, middlemen are involved, and the money is carried as legal tender.

As shown by Nigel Harris (2002) and others, remittances are spent in a variety of ways, with considerable variation between countries. However, almost everywhere, a proportion is invested in land or small enterprises. It has been speculated that every dollar sent back to the Philippines leads to a further three dollars in local growth, either through investment or through boosting local demand.

A fascinating aspect of remittances is their low-key, small-scale character, creating strong ties of commitment, obligation and economic transactions between millions of individuals located sometimes at opposite ends of the globe, without many taking notice. But take a stroll in the Pakistani town of Kharian, and you will notice a significant 'Norwegianization' of the town. People carry plastic bags from Oslo shops, many speak Norwegian, and at least one barber has a faded, framed photo of the late King Olav V in his shop. Most of Norway's Pakistanis hail from the Kharian area, and many travel back and forth as often as time and money allow.

A parallel development to the spectacular growth in remittances, which further contributes to a deterritorialization of trust and moral obligation, is the rapid spread of cellphones since around 1990, and the reduced cost of using them. Vertovec (2004) remarks on the significance of the phonecard (precluding a regular subscription) for the transnational connectedness of ordinary immigrants in Europe and North America. In many poor to middle-income countries, cellphone ownership and use seems to be spreading faster than any other new technology. Horst (2006) reports that in Jamaica, 86 per cent of the population over the age of fifteen has a mobile phone and that, by 2003, three-quarters of all phone traffic was cellular. Before the mid-1990s, Horst reports, telephone communication between Jamaica and the outside world was cumbersome, erratic and expensive. Most Jamaicans relied on phone booths, which were often out of order, and calls tended to be brief and slightly breathless as there were often others waiting to use the phone. As Horst says (her work is in Jamaica, but it is relevant for many places) the cellphone enables people to stay regularly in touch with loved ones overseas, and to negotiate personal relationships as well as financial transactions, to give urgent information (such as a death or illness) and so on. Cheaper and more mobile than e-mail (described along similar lines in Trinidad by Miller and Slater 2000), new generations of cellphones can even be used to send instant images of the newborn baby to the parents at home.

Remittances and phone calls are two ways of staying in touch and they sometimes go together. Horst (2006) writes of an elderly lady in Jamaica who needed a bit of money, who phoned her family overseas and received the amount in one hour. These are some of the networks rarely given much attention in the literatures on either migration or globalization, but which in important ways create and maintain strong webs of transnational commitments worldwide. Most significantly, such networks are interpersonal and based on personal commitment – unlike rather a lot of the other transnational or global networks often considered in research on globalization.

7 FOOTBALL AND GLOBALIZATION

As pointed out by Giulianotti and Robertson (2004), few of the many scholars who write about globalization have studied sport. The recent history of football (soccer), in particular, can serve both as an illustration and as an indication of the extent of transnational interconnectedness.

Football, a sport played to varying degrees in most parts of the world, has British origins but is, unlike cricket, not associated with colonialism. Its rules are easy to learn, it requires no expensive equipment and it can be played in alleys, on lawns, in schoolyards and on open fields. Goalposts can be made from anything – schoolbags and sweaters were standard in my childhood – and the size of the teams is not important. No special skills are required to play football.

As a spectator sport, football also has enormous appeal with its combination of complexity and simplicity, elegance and brute force, its many variations and possibilities for individual players to shine.

This does not in itself explain the global popularity of football nor its failure, so far, to penetrate some of the largest and most populous countries in the world (it is not particularly widespread in India, China or the US). However, in all European and Latin American countries, in most of Africa and in large parts of Asia, football is the single most popular sport. At a transnational level, the game, its tournaments, the ranking of national teams and so on are governed by FIFA. The global turnover in football was estimated, in 2001, at around £250 billion (Giulianotti and Robertson 2004).

Following Robertson (1992), one may say that globalization involves a heightened awareness of the world as an interconnected place, and that processes of globalization tend to be met with *glocalization* (Robertson's term), that is local adaptations of global trends. Both aspects of globalization are clearly present in the football world: international games, at the club or national team level, are prestigious, and fans are increasingly familiar with the football scene in countries other than their own. Yet, teams continue to be locally based and are associated with a home ground and a team mythology. Many teams are invested with political and cultural capital extraneous to the game: Glasgow Rangers is a Protestant team whereas Celtic is Catholic (and the tension between these Scottish teams is played out between Catholics and Protestants in Belfast as well!). Liverpool is associated with the working class, Everton with the middle class. Matches between Barcelona and Real Madrid are symbolic battles over Spanish politics, reflecting the tension between Catalonia and the central power in Madrid.

Increasingly, football has become transnational in a new way. The number of foreign players on major teams has increased steadily. In its standard lineup for the 2006–7 season, Arsenal had only one or two English players (fifteen years earlier, they had just one foreigner), and the Antwerp team Beveren reached the Belgian cup final in 2004 with a team composed almost entirely of players from the Ivory Coast!

Even the changing face of nations in an era of transnational migration is illustrated in football. The French national team that won the 1998 World Cup was led by Zinedine Zidane, a player of Algerian origin, and the team was denounced by the nationalist leader Jean-Marie le Pen as 'not a real French team'. Another example is the Nigerian striker Emmanuel Olisadebe, who played in Poland and was fast-tracked for citizenship to strengthen the Polish national team. Ironically, although Olisadebe remains a Polish citizen, he now plays for the Greek club Panathinaikos.

Fan bases are increasingly becoming transnational as well. Several English football clubs have more registered fans in Norway than even the most popular domestic clubs. Expensive merchandise, ranging from shirts to bedlinen and curtains, is sold worldwide. Some of the richest clubs, like Real Madrid, Bayern München and Manchester United, can indeed be seen as transnational corporations selling goods to fans all over the world. There is a strong glocal element here, in that supporter culture carries different cultural connotations in different localities. Tottenham Hotspur is not associated with the Jewish community of north London outside the UK, nor do most Manchester United supporters in Japan relate to the club's history – they are more interested in its current stars.

Being a football supporter has become more complicated and reflects the interconnectedness and emerging complexity of the contemporary world. Before the 2006 World Cup, I discovered that my son (who was then nine) disapproved of the Swedish striker Zlatan Ibrahimovic. I asked if it had anything to do with the Swedes as such (there has been friendly rivalry between Sweden and Norway for many years, not least in sport) or with Zlatan's controversial personality. I ruled out the possibility that the animosity had anything to do with Zlatan's Yugoslav origins, as my son was too young to have developed xenophobic prejudices. Eventually, it turned out that the problem was that Zlatan played for Juventus, a team my son disapproved of. As a faithful Arsenal fan, my son supported France in the World Cup, since Arsenal's star player Thierry Henry had a pivotal place in the French squad.

The organization of football today involves many cross-cutting ties of loyalty, deterritorialized fandom and global governance (with considerable democratic deficit), but its 'global' dimension is limited, as pointed out by McGovern (2002). The flow of players between countries is far from completely global and deterritorialized; most of it takes place between metropolitan countries and ex-colonies or within a region sharing many cultural characteristics, such as Northern Europe. Clubs remain attached to a semi-sacred place (the home ground) and tend to be domestically owned (with some much-publicized exceptions).

Football also exemplifies economic globalization. As much as 60 per cent of all leather footballs are stitched in the city of Sialkot, north-eastern Pakistan. The workers earn, on an average, the equivalent of £700 a year, twice the average wage in the country. Some of the footballs can cost up to £100 apiece in Europe. Ironically, cricket-addicted Pakistan is one of the countries where football is not a major sport.

Cuban Exceptionalism

A central location in an early, some would say the first, phase of globalization in the sixteenth and seventeenth centuries, following Columbus and the emergent conceptualization of 'the New World', Cuba subsequently became, like the rest of the Caribbean, something of a backwater economically and politically. By the mid-twentieth century, Cuba was a typical Latin American country: politically authoritarian, economically dependent and still based on a plantation system using on relatively simple technology, and dominated by US interests, from investors to mafiosi. Following the 1959 revolution, Cuba severed its ties with the capitalist world, forging a strong ideological, military and economic alliance with the Soviet Union and its East European allies. With the collapse of the so-called Communist bloc around 1990, many predicted that Cuba would follow suit. This was not to happen. At the time of writing, Cuba remains a centralized one-party society with a planned economy, limited civil rights and a very piecemeal and partial integration into the global networks of the early twenty-first century.

Cuban exceptionalism, some would say autonomy, is suggestive of the extent to which much of the rest of the world is enmeshed in a plethora of transnational networks:

- Controlled flow of information. Censorship effectively limits the access to information, including critical information about the state, for the vast majority of Cubans. Internet access is extremely limited, and satellite channels on television are only available in tourist areas.

- Lack of market mechanism in the peso economy. Most Cubans receive their salaries in moneda nacional, a non-convertible currency that enables them to buy goods and services at subsidized prices. A meal in the university canteen at Cienfuegos, for example, costs the equivalent of 2p, a local bus ticket 1p. Prices are fixed by the state rather than through a supply/demand mechanism.

- Limited integration into the world market. Much of Cuba's foreign trade is still (despite the disappearance

8 DELINKING, CHOSEN AND ENFORCED

As many writers on globalization have noted, one particularly visible feature of it is the emergence of strong localist and traditionalist identities. The contrast between a borderless global network society on the one hand and fervent isolationism on the other is like flypaper for journalists and scholars, and book titles like *The Lexus and the Olive Tree* (T. Friedman 1999) and *Jihad vs McWorld* (Barber 1995) are irresistible when the browsing customer in an airport bookshop stumbles across them. There is a simple dialectic to be grasped here: The transnational network economy, and its cultural correlates, create opportunities for some and powerlessness for others. French filmmakers are unhappy with Hollywood's global dominance (which

of the East European market) regulated through bilateral trade agreements with friendly states like Venezuela. The availability of imported goods in the peso sector is limited.

- Limited flow of persons. Cubans are not free to leave their country and obtaining a passport is in most cases impossible.
- Absence of transnational corporations. There is no McDonalds in Cuba, and you'd be hard pressed to find a spare part for your Macintosh laptop in Havana.

There are several cracks and fissures in this system. Two parallel economies operate alongside the planned, subsidy-based peso economy. First, foreigners use the peso convertible, a hard currency with which one may obtain many imported and luxury goods theoretically unavailable to Cubans. Many tourist hotels are joint ventures between the Cuban state and foreign — often Spanish — companies, and 'dollar shops' sell international brands. (But, tellingly, video films aimed at the tourist market are still, in 2006, exclusively in the obsolete VHS format.) Second, a thriving informal economy, operating among Cubans and between Cubans and foreigners, means that many Cubans sell goods and services to tourists (sometimes goods stolen from the state, such as cigars), often in or beyond a legal grey zone — this activity is known as *jineterismo* (hustling) — giving them access to pesos convertible. In spite of this, Cuba remains largely aloof from many of the forms of globalization characterizing most of the world: disparities in wealth are modest compared to other Caribbean and Latin American countries — most private cars are old and either American (pre-1959) or Soviet (pre-1991) — print media are few and censored, television is state controlled, Internet is rare, foreign travel is illegal unless one marries abroad, and so on. Although Cuba is committed to international co-operation through NGOs and the UN system, it has resisted global capitalism and the global information economy surprisingly efficiently, not least when we take its geographical location into account.

is, incidentally, somewhat less than often assumed); pious Muslims are unhappy with images from cable TV and from the London and Paris streets they walked as students; Scandinavians worry about the future of their welfare state in a situation of global economic competition; and indigenous leaders worldwide are concerned to retain a way of life and a culture which at least embody some central features of their tradition. Global capitalism, it is often said, produces both losers and winners, both poverty and wealth. It could be added that even in the cases where it provides increased (measurable) wealth, it can also produce poverty at the cultural or spiritual level. 'We have everything now, but that is all we have,' laments a folksinger who lives in a leafy Oslo suburb where everybody is wired in every conceivable way but few know their neighbours any more and even fewer have the time to read Dostoyevsky, being too busy with their e-mail, meetings and TV. Countermovements against the limitless standardization and homogenization seemingly resulting from globalization can thus be founded in a variety of motivations, but all of them are to do with autonomy at the personal or community level. I shall have much more to say about this in later chapters, but at this point we should note that globalization, even when met with little or no resistance, can usually be described as *glocalization*: the pre-existing, local is fused with global influence; the particular merges with the universal to create something true to the universal grammar of global modernity, but at the same time locally embedded.

Possibly because most of the literature concentrates on the people who are actively part of the process, who make their imprint and contribute to shaping the economy, politics and culture of the planet, a huge part of the world's population is plainly left out of most globalization studies. I have slum dwellers in mind, those fast-growing populations largely comprising people who have moved from rural areas because life was no longer sustainable there.

The extent to which urban slum growth is a result of globalization is debatable. Depletion of agricultural land combined with population growth is one way of describing it. On the other hand, deregulation of national economies (which often have followed the advice of the IMF and reduced the public sector dramatically) has made millions superfluous in the labour force. Mechanization and informatization reduces the need for manpower in the economy, and few states in the Third World have policies effectively preventing slum growth. Mike Davis (2006) presents some shocking figures.

In 2007, for the first time in human history there will be more urban than rural people in the world, and most of the urban growth takes place in poor countries. Cities in the rich countries grow somewhat, but in a slow and fairly controlled way. The growth in poor cities lacks historical precedent. Between 1800 and 1910, the population of London grew by a factor of seven. This sounds dramatic, but in a much shorter period – from 1950 to 2000 – the population in cities like Dhaka, Kinshasa and Lagos has increased *forty times*!

Buenos Aires and Rio de Janeiro were already large cities in the mid-twentieth century, with 4.6 and three million inhabitants, respectively. In 2006, both had around twelve million inhabitants. Cairo has grown, in the same period, from 2.4 million to fifteen million, Delhi from 1.4 to more than eighteen million, Seoul from one to twenty-two million. African cities like Nouakchott and Mogadishu, which were just oases or trading posts a few decades ago, are now home to millions. The Congolese city Mbuji-Mayi has grown from next to nothing to two million in the last decade. Urban slums emerge, especially in China and parts of Africa, in areas where there was initially no urban settlement at all – gigantic slums without a city proper. In Kenya, an incredible 85 per cent of the population growth now takes place in the seething slums of Nairobi and Mombasa.

Certain areas are about to grow into enormous, continuous settlements of cardboard and corrugated iron, with millions upon millions of inhabitants – seen by the authorities as human driftwood – but no plumbing, electricity or police protection. Davis (2006) mentions the 500 kilometre stretch from Rio to São Paolo (pop. 37m.), the central Mexican highlands around Mexico City (estimated to contain half of Mexico's population by 2050), parts of China and the coastal strip from Benin City via Lagos to Accra, which is predicted, in a few years' time, to contain the largest concentration of poverty in the world.

People move to town for a variety of reasons. Traditionally, a main cause, or cluster of causes, has been a combination of relative overpopulation in rural areas and possibilities for work. The 'bright lights' perspective also had its supporters – people left boredom, or so they believed, for excitement. Such explanations may still hold true in parts of China and India, but not in Africa or Latin America, where urban economies have in fact been in decline during the last decades, at the same time as the urban population has doubled several times. An explanation would have to take into account factors such as war, depleted resources as a result of population growth or ruthless modernization (the construction of motorways and resorts for the rich, and so forth), along with a dream of prosperity and work that becomes increasingly unrealistic as the years go by.

The main headache for government and comfortably-off people concerns how to control and contain the slum population, in order to prevent them from spreading, with their rags and stink, into prosperous quarters and commercial centres. In many colonial cities, high-ranking military officers, apparatchiks, politicians and businessmen have joined expatriates from rich countries in taking over the lush residential areas left by the colonials. Increasingly, such suburbs of affluence and freshness are becoming gated communities where nobody is allowed to enter without permission. In parts of Cape Town, electrical fences have now replaced human guards. New forms of apartheid-like exclusion develop as a result of rich people's wish to be left alone with their wealth. They have effectively divorced themselves from greater society in their cosmopolitan, transnational homes.

How do slum dwellers survive at all, given that only a minuscule minority have formal work? The answer is the informal sector (a term coined by Keith Hart, 1973), which is unregistered economic activity. Some make a living by selling each other services, from haircuts and sex to transport and protection; some run little workshops producing tourist trinkets; some grow cannabis or distil alcohol; and some make a living from the rubbish of the rich, be it old furniture or edible things. Many, not least children, are informally employed by large enterprises. They survive, but just barely.

The distance between life in the slums and the rich suburbs grows. The rich have their health centres and shopping malls, their fast food restaurants and private schools (in Ritzer's terms, they have an abundance of nothing, but try to say that to a slum dweller!) and at the weekends they can whisk out to their country houses or resorts on new highways, which are built on land that might have been used for other purposes. They are the beneficiaries of a globalization and a standardization of lifestyles which liberates them from their own countries, connected as they are to the rich world through numerous bridgeheads and networks. In substantial parts of the world, it now appears that nation-building and development 'for the whole people' was something one tried to achieve in the twentieth century, a project now abandoned.

Both at the individual level and at the macro level of states, the *degree of interconnectedness* usually measures the degree of success. This is what counts in the network society. Few individuals who are never sought after either online or by telephone, who rarely leave home and who know nobody beyond a radius of five minutes' walking distance, are successful and thriving in this society. About states, it can be said with even greater confidence that no isolated state is successful in providing material security for its inhabitants or offering them civil rights and personal freedom. The degree of connectedness, and the reach of the connections, indicates the degree of participation in all kinds of contexts. Voluntary delinking, at the individual level, is a luxury indicating affluence; at the level of the state, it is always selective, never comprehensive.

Interconnectedness is, thus, both a central feature of globalization and a way of measuring success in a globalized society. It is beyond doubt that the scope and compass of connections, which are often deterritorialized and transnational, are characteristic of the present era; another question, more difficult to answer, is whether connectedness has been similarly valued in earlier periods? The answer seems to be that, at the individual level, wide-ranging personal networks and mutual ties of obligation would mainly be an asset – not least for people engaged in trade and politics. At the societal level, trade and openness to the world would also be profitable in most cases, but not always. In an influential essay on some of the dimensions of globalization, Appadurai (1990) argues that the globalization processes are *disjunctive* in that they move along different axes and with different ends. He distinguishes between ethnoscapes, mediascapes, technoscapes, finanscapes and ideoscapes as five relatively separate fields affected by, and affecting, globalization. Appadurai argues that global flows take place through these five distinctive dimensions, which collide and enter into conflict with one another. The degree of transnational interconnectedness varies along such dimensions (a country may be financially transnational, but ethnically parochial, for example), so that interconnectedness is rarely an either-or issue, but a question that needs a more considered answer: What kind of interconnectedness is under investigation? What is the underlying motivation? What are the social consequences? Individuals, groups and states all have restrictions imposed on their connections with the outside world, deliberately or not. These restrictions are often associated with movement of goods and people, to which we now turn.

Chapter Summary

- Through trade, communication and movement, most of the world is increasingly interconnected, with political, economic and cultural consequences.
- Economic interconnectedness develops not only through huge transnational corporations, but also in a small and medium-scale enterprises spreading their assets, investments and collaboration internationally.
- Technological interconnectedness through, for example, ICT does not necessarily mean enhanced interaction; for example, local languages often predominate.
- Mass migration has led to new patterns of transnational interconnectedness, linking people interpersonally, often through kinship, across continents.
- The growth of the NGO system indicates an increased interdependence and integration of a different kind from the economic and technological connectedness.

5 MOVEMENT

Nowadays we are all on the move.

Zygmunt Bauman

INTRODUCTION

Reminiscing about what became of the people who used to live in his Kumasi neighbourhood when he was a child, the philosopher Kwame Anthony Appiah says:

> Eddie, from across the street, who never finished school, called to wish me a Happy New Year from Japan; Frankie, my cousin from next door to Eddie, lives in England; Mrs Effah still lives next door, but visits her children in the United States; even my mother and sister have moved across the city (Appiah 2003: 195).

As pointed out by Jan Aart Scholte (2005: 65), 'methodological territorialism has had a pervasive and deep hold on the conventions of social research; thus globalization (when understood as the spread of supranationality) implies a major reorientation of approach.'

Scholte, a political scientist, argues that researchers have tended to take territorial units for granted in their studies, seeing the world 'through the lens of territorial geography', assuming that societies take a territorial form. Although Scholte and others (for example, Urry 2000) try to develop methodologies for the study of non-territorial, or deterritorialized, phenomena – diasporic groups, tourism, the Internet, financial capital – they do not proclaim the end of territoriality. Scholte stresses that 'the end of territorial*ism* does not mean the 'end of territorial*ity*' (Scholte 2005: 76). However, in an interconnected world, few territories can be *merely* territories, and few if any territories can be *bounded* territories. They become territories interlinked with, and responding to, processes taking place far beyond their limits, and therefore *reterritorialization*, the attempt to fix and stabilize a place, a country or a region, is itself a product of its own dialectical negation, that is deterritorialization.

Although it sounds hyperbolic to say that 'we are all on the move', it is true in several senses that movement is characteristic of contemporary globalization. Tourists, business and conference travellers, refugees and migrants: there are more of them than ever before. There is a sense in which boundaries that may have been considered firm and reliable in the mid-twentieth century are dissolving. Anthropologists are no less uneasy than geographers when confronted with the seemingly unbounded (or at least unevenly bounded) cultures of today, but many follow the lead of Appadurai (1996), Hannerz (1992), J. Friedman (1994), Kearney (1995) and others in refashioning their concept of culture to fit a more complex, interrelated and paradoxical reality. Sociologists conceptualize a 'sociology of movement' (Urry 2000), and political scientists are busy discussing human rights and transnational politics. Whether posterity will judge these tendencies in social theory as fads or ripples, or whether they constitute something like a paradigm shift in the social sciences, we cannot know. Less risky is the assertion that *movement* has to be a key concept of globalization.

I TRANSNATIONAL MIGRATION

Migration is one of the central facts of transnational processes (see Schiller et al. 1992 for a pioneering contribution). Those who trace globalization back to the beginning of the modern era (around 1500 – see, for example, Wolf 1982; Wallerstein 2004) emphasize European colonization of the New World and the Transatlantic slave trade as constitutive events. Those who go even further back (for instance J. Friedman 1992; Chase-Dunn and Hall 1997) stress not just large-scale trade and cultural standardization as features of the Roman Empire, but also the movement of people from Italy to the Iberian peninsula, Gaul and elsewhere. This is also true of pre-modern empires outside Europe, such as the Azteks in Mesoamerica and the Han in China.

Contemporary globalization is characterized by several streams of people: a small trickle of North Atlantic expatriates living temporarily or semi-permanently in the south as diplomats, businessmen or aid workers, and much more substantial streams of people from southern countries to other southern countries (South Africa is a magnet in southern-central Africa; Morocco is a transit country for hundreds of thousands of sub-Saharan Africans hoping to get into Europe, and so on) and from south to north. In the US Canada and Australia, immigration has been seen as a normal process since their inception as settler societies. In European countries, the situation is different and, as is well known, debates over migration policy and the integration of immigrants into the majority societies are omnipresent and cover everything from immigrants' voting patterns to gender roles and discrimination in the labour market.

It should be pointed out, however, that although migration has changed the face of Western cities in recent decades, the proportion of migrants (people living outside their country of birth) is much lower now than it was in the early twentieth century. Although more people live outside their country of birth today than earlier in the history of the state (Papastergiadis 2000), only 3 per cent of the world's population are immigrants today, whereas the proportion in 1913 was around 10 per cent (Cohen 2006).

Migration can be an unsettling, confusing and frustrating experience, especially if it is prompted by 'push' factors rather than 'pull' factors. Immigrants are often ostracized by the majority and denied full civil rights by governments. Many respond by devising both local and transnational strategies strengthening the coherence of their local community and networks, often based on ethnicity or religion, as well as their ties to the countries of origin. Remittances and telecommunications as ways of maintaining moral and economic ties have been discussed earlier; it should be noted that migrant minorities pursue many other strategies as well. Many migrants in Europe reconnect with the homeland through marriage, usually by arranging to move the spouse to the European country. Some send their children to school in the home country for shorter or longer periods. Yet others are involved in long-distance political activities (see below).

Transnational connections among migrants are often economically important. A study of Senegalese Wolof in Emilia Romagna (northern Italy) by Bruno Riccio (1999) demonstrates several important features of transnational entrepreneurship. Wolof are traditionally associated with trade in West Africa, and they have successfully adapted their skills to function transnationally, spanning Senegalese and European markets in their business flows. Riccio argues that in a manner similar to the Hausa of Ibadan, Wolof in Italy are morally and socially bound by their allegiance to Muslim brotherhoods in Senegal (the Mouride) but he also points out that without a strong organization of Wolof wholesalers based in Italy offering not only goods but also training of itinerant salesmen, the individual Wolof peddler would have been chanceless.

The Wolof trade system studied by Riccio functions in both directions. Traders live in Italy part of the year and in Senegal part of the year, and the goods offered for sale in the Senegalese markets range from hi-fi equipment and other electronic goods to the trader's own second-hand clothes. Although Riccio takes pains to describe the variations in the circumstances of migration, an unambiguous pattern emerges from his material, which shows that Wolof migrants to Italy are positioned in Italian society in a unique way, due to particular features of their culture and local organization in Senegal. Somewhat like Gujerati traders in London (Tambs-Lyche 1980), they draw on pre-existing social and cultural resources in developing their economic niche under new circumstances.

Transnational micro-economies have become very widespread during recent decades; and migration must increasingly be envisioned as a transnational venture rather than as a one-way process resulting in segregation, assimilation or integration in the receiving society. The economics of transnationalism can be observed in Congolese *sapeurs* (J. Friedman 1990) flaunting their wealth in Brazzaville following a frugal period of hard work in Paris, in the informal *hawala* banking system whereby Somali refugees send remittances to relatives, in the flow of goods into and out of immigrant-owned shops in any European city, and most certainly in thousands of local communities, from Kerala to Jamaica, which benefit from the work of locals working overseas. Seen from a global structural perspective, this kind of transnational economics can easily be regarded as a vertical ethnic division of labour whereby the exploitative systems of colonialism are continued; seen from the perspective of the local community, it may equally well be seen as a much-needed

From Diasporas to Super-diversity

Unlike the situation in a city like London as late as around 1990, when most immigrants came from ex-colonies, the city's immigrants now truly come from everywhere. Described recently as 'the world in one city', London may be exceptionally diverse regarding the breadth and numbers of its residents of foreign origin, but the tendency described by Steven Vertovec (2006) with reference to London can also be seen elsewhere in the world. While people from 179 countries were present in London according to the 2001 Census – an impressive number – as a matter of fact, 124 languages are spoken only in the southern Oslo suburb of Holmlia!

Foreigners resident in a country are classified according to their circumstances: they are either refugees or economic immigrants, students or tourists, diplomats or spouses of citizens. In recent years, such classificatory schemes have increasingly been seen as unsatisfactory. Contemporary flows of people into the great (and not so great) cities of the world include people who cannot easily be classified as either this or that: students who have stayed on, getting a boyfriend or girlfriend and a McJob; tourists who 'forgot' to return; Polish seasonal workers, legal or not; visitors who are neither quite jobseekers nor exactly not jobseekers. There is an increased degree of imagination in the current movement of people, from Nigerian football players and prostitutes to fake chemical engineers, young brides and grooms brought by established immigrants from the home country, huge trade delegations and north Europeans who settle seasonally in the Mediterranean. It is sometimes said by Lithuanians that cities like source of wealth; and seen from the perspective of the individual, it entails a new set of risks and opportunities.

Many migrant populations are forced to establish webs of security and trust independently of the state in which they live, creating stable minorities with distinct identities. Thus, globalization and migration presents challenges to the state from within (see Hammar et al. 1997). As cultural similarity as a normative basis for society becomes unrealistic, social cohesion at the level of the territorial state becomes less likely, and the normative and cultural basis of the state needs to be redefined.

Another aspect of migration is border control. The national borders of rich countries are increasingly becoming militarized, physical walls and fences are raised and the density of patrol boats and armed forces along borders is growing (Aas, in press). Simultaneously, prison populations in the same countries are swelling with immigrants and other foreigners. Resembling gated communities in more than one respect, the rich countries try to stem and direct incoming transnational flows, sifting 'tourists' from 'vagabonds', to use Bauman's (1998) terms.

Vilnius and Kaunas are virtually emptied of people between 20 and 35 in the summer months as they are all in the West, working or looking for work. As we have seen in Poland, there has for years been a shortage of construction workers, since many work semi-permanently in Germany, Sweden and other high-salary countries – in most cases without being immigrants in those countries.

Vertovec notes that whereas most of the immigration into the UK before the 1990s was of Commonwealth origin (similarly, most immigration into France came from its ex-colonies), immigrants now come from everywhere – rich, middle-income and poor countries. In London, there were in 2005 more than 40 nationalities numbering more than ten thousand. The diversity is staggering and impossible to describe in simplifying

terms. Within each group, there is great variation in people's immigration status (some are refugees, some spouses, some students, some undocumented and so on), their educational level and their way of integrating into British society. The era of the settled, stable, spatially concentrated diasporic population – Bangladeshi in Tower Hamlets, Jamaicans in Brixton – is gone. In its stead, there is now a dynamic, forever changing ethnic mosaic in a city like London, where some are there to stay, others to commute, yet others to leave for greener pastures or just home, wherever that is. The new situation, familiar in many other cities as well, puts pressure on local government to provide services adapted to a super-diverse and shifting situation with extremely heterogeneous neighbourhoods and hugely varied needs.

2 OUTSOURCING THE NATION-STATE?

Nation-states are often seen as the victims of globalization, but they may sometimes profit from it by deterritorializing some of their activities. Let me give a couple of examples from the country where I live.

Bits of Norway are being exported to places where it is more pleasant or interesting to be. Students, pensioners and various service providers migrate seasonally, some permanently, to more temperate places. The numbers of retired Norwegians who spend part of the year in southern Europe (especially the Costa del Sol) is rising. They do not necessarily have any interest in Spain as such, and make sure to get their *Aftenposten* every morning, participate in Norwegian clubs and organizations, get Norwegian nurses and dentists to look after their medical needs, and have even succeeded in opening Norwegian schools in their preferred areas. Norwegian students, for their part, increasingly do part of their study in other countries, Australia being the country of preference currently – not because of the quality of their universities; Australian universities are, on the whole, neither better nor worse than their Norwegian counterparts – but for other, obvious reasons to do with climate, excitement, cultural similarities and expectations of a higher quality of life. Some even bring their teachers and reading lists with them; in March 2006, I taught a group of young Norwegians a course on Latin American history and globalization in Cuba. They left Norway in January and returned in late May for their exams.

A different, but similar phenomenon is the transmigration engaged in by many immigrants to Norway and their descendants. Spending part of the year in their country of origin if they have the opportunity to, many immigrants have developed attachments and obligations towards two places in disparate countries, and it can be argued that certain parts of Pakistani Punjab have been just as Norwegianized as the Norwegian-dominated villages in southern Spain.

A second, economically more important kind of outsourcing consists in making others do the work. A rich country like Norway relies increasingly on foreigners doing the work. A few years ago, the shops suddenly began to fill up with all kinds of goods; everything was really cheap and it was all made in China. Simultaneously, growing numbers of seasonal workers from Poland and the Baltic states make major contributions to the economy – in western Europe so many Poles work in construction that there is a shortage of construction workers in Poland, where one now has to subcontract Ukrainian entrepreneurs to get buildings finished. (One wonders what they will eventually do in Ukraine – the answer is probably Chinese firms.)

These are some of the things a nation-state can use globalization for, without losing its integrity as a nation-state. The question is how long these kinds of processes can go on before new, more complex allegiances are being forged.

3 TOURISM

The inhabitants of Norway in 1850 never went on holiday. Some of the very rich went on once-in-a-lifetime tours of Europe, some from the privileged classes studied in Copenhagen or Berlin, and thousands of sailors travelled abroad because it was their job. Half a century later, this began to change. The imported idea of the seaside resort materialized, and mountain trips dear to the emerging middle-class nationalism began to resemble tourism in the modern sense, featuring the exotic (local peasants) and the magnificent (the mountains). Half a century later again, the package trip to the Mediterranean was introduced, but most Norwegians still spent their holidays (which they were now entitled to) at home or in another Scandinavian country.

Similar developments took place earlier in a few other countries, notably Britain, where 48 London coaches a day served the seaside in Brighton as early as the summer months of the 1830s, and the package trip was invented by Thomas Cook as early as 1844. Nevertheless, the emergence of mass tourism has happened, and has unfolded, fairly synchronically, in the rich countries. Whereas my parents spent their summer holidays in the family cottage when they were young, I went to southern Europe with my friends on an Interrail ticket, and those who are twenty years younger than me would travel to South America or Thailand. This illustrates the evolution of tourism, from local to regional to global, as it has unfolded in most parts of the rich world.

The word 'tourist' was still a recent invention in the mid-twentieth century. Due to economic growth and technological changes (including, notably, cheap flights), the tourist industry has grown steadily since the 1950s, making it the possibly largest economic sector in the world. By the mid-1990s, 7 per cent of the global workforce, around 230 million persons, were employed in tourism (Löfgren 1999: 6). Tourist organizations predict that in the year 2020, 1.6 billion people will make a trip abroad. The Mediterranean area, the most popular foreign destination for north Europeans, received about six million tourists annually in 1955. In 2005, the number was 220 million, expected by the World Tourist Organization to grow to 350 million by 2020 (unless something unexpected happens, such as paleness becoming fashionable again, or rapid climate change making the heat unbearable in summer). Most tourists in the Mediterranean area, Löfgren (1999: 187) comments, 'have to get used to vacationing in an eternal construction site.'

Global tourism can be interpreted along several lines. One is homogenization, industrialization and mass production along the lines described by George Ritzer in *The McDonaldization of Society* (Ritzer 1993). Leafing through the free catalogues distributed by the large tour operators, it is difficult to notice where the Spanish section ends and the Brazilian section begins. There is a global grammar of package tourism which entails that tourist destinations have to conform to a minimal set of requirements. If the destination is of the sun-and-sand type, nightclubs, snorkelling trips, swimming pools, playgrounds and charming, open-air markets are *de rigueur*. Food is either 'international' or modified local. Tennis courts and minigolf are ubiquituous. If the destination is a city, standardized 'sights' (the Rijksmuseum, the Sacre Cœur, the Tower of London) are featured along with advice on shopping opportunities. Hotels are classified according to an international ranking system.

Another perspective on global tourism would emphasize its glocal dimension, blending local culture, food and music with the common denominators required by the global grammar of tourism. Toilets and bathrooms, the tourist staff's language skills and food preparation, to mention a few dimensions, cannot be tampered with too much within this grammar, which ensures that any tourist destination should in principle be accessible to middle-class travellers from anywhere. However, local

How American is Globalization?

Every country in the world (with the probable exception of the US) has its own domestic debate about Americanization and, almost everywhere, the middle classes and establishment media worry about it. They write and say that Hollywood and American cable companies dominate on TV and in the cinema, that the fast food giants invade and transform the national food culture, that American telecom and computer corporations dictate the new media, that bad American pop music is ubiquitous and that transnational companies based in the US dominate the world economy.

To what extent are these assumptions correct? Take television first. It is true that American soaps and sitcoms are broadcast in many countries, and CNN is available in an incredible number of hotel rooms. But the most popular TV programmes are nearly always locally produced. Besides, Mexican and Brazilian soap operas

(telenovelas) are more popular than the American ones in many countries, especially in the Third World.

A similar statement could be made with respect to fast food. Yes, McDonald's restaurants are astonishingly widespread, but they rarely have a market-dominant position. In a city like Avignon, there is one McDonald's and about 200 other restaurants and bars. In Japan, several chains, including Yoshinoya, which serves traditional Japanese food, have more restaurants than McDonald's. McDonald's isn't even the largest fast food corporation in the world. That position is held by the British corporation Compass, which owns Burger King, Sbarro and other chains. Even 7-Eleven, that archetype of Americanization, is owned by Japanese.

What about American corporations, don't they, at least, dominate the world? In fact, no. They dominate in the US, but not many other places. Volkswagen sells flavour is sometimes considerable and is indeed often a main attraction. Along the lush and picturesque Gudbrandsdal valley of central southern Norway, numerous converted farms and newly built guesthouses in an old-fashioned style are calibrated to attract tourists (many of them Norwegian-Americans) in search of 'the authentic'. So staff are paid to wear traditionalist clothes, to serve dishes rarely seen on Norwegian dinner tables, and to play fiddle music. In general, the cultural dimension of tourism has become more and more pronounced as the number of tourists grows and their interests diversify. The folklore show has become a staple in many 'exotic' tourist locations, and in some areas (such as South Africa and Indonesia) tourists' group tours to real villages or real townships have become an important source of income to people living there.

Tourist destinations are at least two places at one and the same time: A holiday destination and a local community. People from Benidorm live in a Spanish town, whereas tourists are on holiday in southern Europe, a place with totally different

---

more cars in China than all the American car makers combined. Toyota is the number three car maker in the USA, making one suspect that the Nipponization of the US is more tangible than the Americanization of Japan!

On the other hand, a quarter of the world's 100 largest non-financial enterprises are American. Yet, most of them have their main assets in the US itself. Whereas the British telecom company Vodafone has 80 per cent of its assets overseas, the figure for McDonald's is only 40 per cent.

In some areas, American companies dominate the world economy. This is the case with oil companies like Exxon, airplane factories like Boeing, and computing companies like Microsoft, Dell and Apple. In the media and entertainment world, American giants like Time Warner and Disney retain a strong position, although Sony may be the world's largest media company and the Dutch company Polygram the largest music company.

Globalization is, in other words, not Americanization even if we restrict our scope to consumer habits and economic flows. In some areas, the US is in fact less globalized than many other countries. Far fewer Americans than South Koreans have Internet at home, and regarding mobile telephony, the US has been lagging behind for years. Americans travel abroad far less than Europeans — most don't even have a passport — and the international standard metre of 1889, described in an earlier chapter, is stored safely in Sèvres and is unlikely to cross the Atlantic any time soon. (See Marling 2006 for further details.)

connotations. In many popular tourist destinations, not least in the Mediterranean, locals are shocked and outraged at what they see as a hedonistic culture of permissiveness, especially among the young vacationers, coming from northern Europe. A colleague in Cyprus was visibly relieved, but also expressed concern, when I told him that the young Scandinavians who engage routinely in casual sex and take recreational drugs in the clubs dotting the island's south coast would never dare to behave in the same way at home.

As always, there are exceptions to this rule. Cancun, on the Caribbean coast of Mexico, was non-existent as late as the mid-1970s. By early 2007 it had about half a million inhabitants, virtually all of whom are employed directly or indirectly in the tourism industry. It is a place with no history and no collective identity, established because of the need among US tour operators to find a new appropriate destination – Florida was filling up – four hours or less by plane from the main US cities. (Slightly south of Cancun, a town apparently designed for European tourists was developed, namely Playa del Carmen, with smaller hotels, less traffic and pedestrian streets with quaint shops and bars.)

The tourist, as described by Urry (1990) and Löfgren (1999), is a skilled vacationer who knows the cultural codes and rules regulating the role of the tourist. However, tourism has diversified, and today it would probably be correct to speak of a plurality of tourisms. 'Anti-tourism' of the generic backpacker kind, for example, has been institutionalized and standardized for decades, so that popular 'alternative' travel guidebooks like the Lonely Planet and Rough Guide series can be bought in every airport or bookshop, giving sound advice as to which local bus to take to see temples off the beaten track and which guesthouses to avoid because staff tends to steal from the guests.

4 THE TOURIST AND THE REFUGEE

Tourism entails leisure and easy, laid-back consumption. Adrian Franklin (2004) has suggested that city centres are now being redesigned in order to enable people to be 'tourists at home', with a proliferation of sleek buildings, coffee-bars, riverside or seaside promenades lined with restaurants and so on. Lash and Urry (1993: 258) also suggest that while some tourists make an effort to mingle with the locals, many local residents behave like tourists in using tourist facilities in their own countries. In deeply class-divided societies, tourist areas may need to be physically closed off from the rest of society in order to avoid friction and for the sake of security. The beaches in Jamaica's Montego Bay are patrolled by armed guards, as is the Cape Town waterfront.

Bauman phrases an important difference like this: 'One difference between those "high up" and those "low down" is that the first may leave the second behind – but not vice versa' (Bauman 1998: 86). Although most people in the world continue to lead most of their lives near the place where they grew up, some are free to travel on vacation (or business), whereas others are forced to leave their homes as refugees or economic migrants. According to figures from the United Nations High Commission for Refugees (UNHCR), there were 185 million international migrants in 2005. To this may be added tens of millions of internal migrants, not least in populous countries like China and India. The number of international refugees grew from two million in 1975 to 15 million in 1995, but decreased to less than ten million in 2004. However, the number of internally displaced persons, more difficult to count, is estimated to be tens of millions.

The contrast between the tourist and the refugee is stark. The tourist can travel anywhere or almost anywhere with a minimum of friction; the refugee is interrogated at every international border and is likely to be turned away. The tourist moves in a 'third culture' where everybody has a smattering of English, and can easily buy everything he needs. The refugee is usually penniless and dependent on charity, and often encounters serious problems of understanding with the locals due to lack of a shared language. The tourist, of course, is free to leave any moment, while the refugee is ordered to and fro. Tellingly, the tourist, always short of time at home, makes a virtue of reducing his or her speed and limiting the daily activities while on vacation, and the refugee's life is full of slow, empty time where nothing happens. Both exemplify the predominance of movement in the contemporary world, and between them, the refugee and the tourist give an accurate depiction of the uneven distribution of resources in the globalized world.

5 LONG-DISTANCE NATIONALISM

The 'multiple identities that arise from globalization, especially as more and more people live in more than one country' (Castles and Davidson 2000: 87) often result in hyphenated identities, which have been especially pronounced in the New World. On a visit to Canada around 1990, I noticed that my Canadian friends spoke of each other as 'Ukrainian', 'Portuguese' and so on. This was not meant to question their national loyalty, but indicated something about origins and networks. Their Canadianness was taken for granted; the predicate before the implicit hyphen suggested, if anything, that having a mixed identity was legitimate.

For decades, it was believed in North America that immigrant minorities would generally become assimilated, that their markers of difference would gradually fade away. At least this was assumed to be the case of immigrants with European origins; with people of 'non-standard appearance' (blacks, Latin Americans, Asians), it was another story. Nonetheless, since the 1960s social scientists and others have discovered that ethnic and national identities did not vanish – indeed, that they were in some cases strengthened. Even third- and fourth-generation Irish or Danes considered themselves somehow as 'Irishmen' and 'Danes', often even without having visited the country of their ancestors. Although they became culturally assimilated, the identity remained attached to origins.

Anderson (1992) coined the term *long-distance nationalism* to describe some political implications of continued allegiance to a country, or region, where one either no longer lives or indeed has never lived. Some of the older minorities in the US, such as Irish and Jews, have members who have for many years been actively involved in politics in Ireland and Israel, often supporting nationalist movements and trying to influence American policy through lobbying and strategic voting. However, the practices of long-distance nationalism have become much more widespread in recent years, due to

- the great increase in the numbers of immigrants; and
- the increased facility in swift communication.

To take a few examples: the Hindu nationalists of the BJP in India (Bharatya Janata Party, the 'Indian People's Party') have depended crucially on financial and moral support from 'NRIs' (non-resident Indians), many in north America. During the break-up and subsequent wars of Yugoslavia, Yugoslavs in countries like Sweden and Australia began to emphasize their *ethnic* identities as Bosnians, Serbs and Croats, and made active contributions to the war. Many Tamils in western Europe are involved in the independence struggle in Sri Lanka – indeed, for many, their potential contributions to the Tamil Eelam's secession attempt is their main cause for being abroad (Fuglerud 1999).

Anderson's only extended example illustrates the case well. He speaks about a Sikh living in Toronto, who actively supports the Khalistani movement in Indian Punjab, a violent movement that has often targeted civilians in terrorist attacks. This man does not participate in Canadian political life, but 'lives, through e-mail, by long-distance nationalism' (Anderson 1992: 11, see also R. Cohen 1997: 110–15). Asked by a fellow Sikh why he does not move back, he explains that it is too dangerous and that he prefers his children to grow up in peaceful Toronto.

In Anderson's words

> his political participation is directed towards an imagined heimat in which he
> does not intend to live, where he pays no taxes, where he cannot be arrested,

where he will not be brought before the courts – and where he does not vote; in effect, a politics without responsibility or accountability. (Anderson 1992: 11)

Yet at the same time, this kind of politics is, it may seem, an inevitable outcome of intensified transnational connections. Sometimes, as Anderson's and my examples above suggest, the diasporic populations, nostalgic for the imagined authenticity of their childhood (or that of their grandparents) support cultural purity movements opposed to 'faceless modernization', political compromises and cultural hybridization. As a result, they often support – from the safety of exile – militant nationalist groups. On the other hand, there are also examples of long-distance nationalist movements with other political agendas. Arab, Iranian and South Asian feminist groups working from exile in western Europe to improve the conditions for women in the home country.

6 NOSTALGIA

When something moves, simple dialectical negation suggests that we should ask what doesn't. Quite obviously, most of the world's inhabitants stay put, even if the circumstances of their lives change because of globalization's direct or indirect impact. This is what Bauman means when he says that 'we are all on the move these days'. At the same time, the age of fast transnational movement has also proven to be the age of nostalgia and traditionalism, which could be defined as a modern ideology promoting tradition. As Giddens (1991) says, complex contemporary societies tend to be *post-traditional*. This does not mean that they have done away with all tradition, but that traditions must be defended actively because they can no longer be taken for granted. In the post-traditional world, dormant traditions are resurrected, adapted to fit new circumstances, commercialized and politicized.

As I write these lines, Norway has just celebrated its Constitution Day (17 May), and never before have there been as many folk costumes in town as this year. More than 90 per cent of the population celebrate 17 May, and more than half of the women wear folk dresses (*bunader*). The number of men, although much lower, is also on the rise. In my childhood, three decades ago, which unfolded in a less intensively globalized world, folk dresses were rarely seen in the urban centres of south-eastern Norway. Now, consider the fact that a short while before the annual 17 May celebrations, Norwegians had, like other West Europeans, been debating the question of whether or not to legislate against the use of headscarves (*hijabs*) among Muslim immigrant women. Again, a couple of decades ago, *hijabs* were hardly ever seen among Muslim immigrant women in Europe. Even today, some young Muslim women wear the *hijab* against their father's wish.

In all likelihood, few of the very many women (and men) sporting neo-traditionalist garb on Constitution Day would have reflected on the parallel between the rise of visible identity markers among minorities and in the majority. And one would have to be a social scientist interested in globalization to see these markers of difference not as a 'natural' expression of a 'natural' identity, nor as a simple reaction against globalization, but as *one of its most common reflexive forms*. If anything, globalization at the level of social identity is tantamount to a re-negotiation of social identities, their boundaries and symbolic content. Nobody can give an unequivocal, uncontroversial definition of what it means to be a Berliner, a Malaysian or a Norwegian any more, but this does not necessarily mean that these identities are going away. Some of them are in fact strengthened, invested with new or old symbolic content; some wane to the benefit of others; some are enlarged or shrink, some become transnational and others remain attached to place. Just as a fish is totally uninterested in water as long as it swims happily around – it is even unlikely to be aware of the existence of water – most people don't think twice about those of their identities that can be taken for granted. But the moment you drag the poor creature out of the sea, be it on a hook or in a net, it immediately develops an intense interest in water; what the water means to it, how it is essential for its survival, and – not least – the peculiar nature of water. Had fish been equipped with an ability to ponder, a great number of short-lived (and doubtless post-structuralist) theories about water would have been sketched in haste, in maritime surroundings, every day. In the case of humans, not only are the national, regional and local identities contested and challenged but it is becoming increasingly difficult to defend absolutist views of gender and kinship identities as well. Place – that is to say a fixed, stable, meaningful space – is becoming a scarce and flexible resource. Maintaining a predictable and secure group identity is hard work in a world of movement, but it is being undertaken, very often successfully.

Chapter Summary

- Globalization involves accelerated and intensified movement of people, objects and ideas, not only from north to south but in every direction.
- Movement nonetheless reflects and tends to reproduce global power discrepancies.
- Although there is currently enormous attention to migration in the West, a far greater percentage of humanity were migrants a hundred years ago than today.
- Contemporary migration is not a finite process, but usually involves enduring transnational ties.
- Forms of human mobility enhanced by and contributing to globalization include, among other things, migration, tourism, business travel, student mobility, crime and even forms of 'transhumance', which includes the seasonal migrations of the wealthy in cold climates to warmer places and seasonal migrant labour.

6 MIXING

The battleground of the twenty-first century will pit fundamentalism against cosmopolitan tolerance.

Anthony Giddens, *Runaway World: How Globalization is Reshaping our Lives*

INTRODUCTION

Some years ago, I had the pleasure of interviewing the author Vikram Seth, who had then just published his epic novel from the early 1950s in India, *A Suitable Boy*. As it happens, we spoke extensively about cultural mixing – his main characters were to varying degrees 'Westernized', yet remained distinctively Indian in their values and way of life. As we spoke, the waitress arrived with a tray, pots and cups. Taking his first sip, Seth sputtered and exclaimed that he had been served a mixture of tea and coffee! Must be horrible, I opined, but Seth insisted that he saw the concoction as a new, exciting mixture.

Mixing is always a result of movement, but repulsion and encapsulation are also possible outcomes. This chapter looks at both sides of the coin – cosmopolitanism and hybridity on the one hand, withdrawal and boundary-marking on the other. First of all, we should make it clear that the cultural dynamics of globalization cannot be seen as 'Westernization' *tout court*, but must be understood as a multidirectional and truly complex process (Amselle 2001, Appadurai 1996, Hannerz 1996). Second, we should keep in mind that there is no such thing as a 'pure' culture. Mixing has always occurred, although its speed and intensity are higher than before. Third, the identity politics positing cultural purity as an alternative to mixing are direct reactions to the mixing. Puritanism, thus, is a consequence of perceived impurity.

In earlier chapters, I have presented views on globalization that suggest that there is a drive towards homogeneity, but I have also emphasized that

■ there is reflexive resistance to this, resulting in glocal forms blending the particular and the universal;

- globalization processes are partial and are unable to transform local cultures totally; and
- large segments of the world's population are affected only indirectly or not at all by globalization processes.

Yet nobody denies that mixing takes place, in language, food habits, customs and so on, in many ways and in every country of the world. Sometimes, cultural impulses from two or several distinct groups mix to create something new; sometimes, the universalist drive of globalization processes mixes with local cultures to produce a glocal version of the universal. Arguing against the belief in a fast global integration, Bayart says that it 'is the Islamists who introduced intellectual categories of the economy into the Muslim world. It is the healers, sorcerers, and kin who speak the market in Central Africa. It is the families of the Chinese diaspora who unify the economic space of East Asia' (Bayart 2003: 334).

Arguing against the theorists of hybridity and creolization as products of globalization, Amselle (2001: 22) favours a view according to which cultures have always mixed and proposes that 'all societies are mixed and thus that mixing is the product of entities which are already mixed, thus sending the idea of an original purity to oblivion' (my translation).

Postcolonialism and the Power of Definition

For a newly independent country, taking over ownership of factories, mines and fields is fairly straightforward, argues the Kenyan author Ngugi wa Thiong'o; what is much more difficult is decolonizing the mind (Ngugi 1986). In his essays, Ngugi relates how he, as a boy growing up in colonial Kenya, was taught about daffodils and snowflakes, Shakespeare and the Tudors, but nothing about African geography or history. Liberating oneself from such an involuntary appropriation of worlds other than one's own is a chief concern in the body of fiction and theory called postcolonial.

Colonialism was a global enterprise, the British Empire a political entity 'where the sun never set', and

postcolonialism is global as well, but moving in the opposite direction, from south to north, in a series of attempts to reclaim some of the power of definition that was lost through generations of colonialism.

Postcolonial studies, a new academic subdiscipline, is often traced to the publication of Edward Said's *Orientalism* (1978), a hugely influential book which criticized European scholars and writers in the colonial era for depicting 'the Orient' in stereotypical and prejudiced ways. However, the debt to the Martiniquan doctor Frantz Fanon and his *Black Skin, White Masks* (1986 [1952]) is usually acknowledged. Fanon showed how imperialism affected the mentality and desires

However, as every serious anthropologist working within the emerging globalization paradigm would stress, 'no total homogenization of systems of meaning and expression has occurred, nor does it appear likely that there will be one any time soon' (Hannerz 1990: 237). Global culture 'is marked by an organization of diversity rather than by a replication of uniformity... But the world has become one network of social relationships, and between its different regions there is a flow of meaning as well as of people and goods' (Hannerz 1990: 237).

Elsewhere, Hannerz has also said that the 'recent confluence of separate and quite different traditions' does not 'mean that these ... cultural currents in themselves have been 'pure', or 'homogeneous', or 'bounded'' (Hannerz 1996: 67).

This is important. Accelerated mixing does not imply a prior 'pristine' state of clearly bounded cultures. Granted that cultural mixing is a common, usually undramatic phenomenon in the contemporary world, we need to look more closely at some of the concepts used to describe the process of mixing. They do not necessarily refer to the same thing.

Variation within any group is considerable, and cultural flows across boundaries ensure that mixing, in the contemporary world, is a continuous possibility or reality. However, the impression sometimes given that 'everything' seems to be in continuous flux, that an infinity of opportunities seem to be open and that no

of black people, making them reject their own histories and experiences and yearn for 'a little bit of whiteness'.

The project of postcolonialism consists, simply put, in developing and promoting the worlds of experience silenced by the dominant or hegemonic groups. Some postcolonial writers, like Ngugi and the Kurdish author Mehmed Uzun, even strive to develop vernaculars as literary languages, but many write in the metropolitan languages, thereby creating a dilemma that is often discussed: how can the imperialist vehicles of communication be used to denounce imperialism?

Many contemporary writers see a link between the quest for liberation and autonomy among the dispossessed of the world, and the need to tell new stories depicting hitherto silenced experiences and rehabilitating life-worlds and social milieux which have formerly either been ignored or depicted as backward and primitive. A global democratization of communication must arguably include not only equal access to technology, but also a fair distribution of the right to speak and the right to be heard.

groups, cultural identities or ethnic categories are fixed, is caused by a conflation of discrete phenomena:

First: strong identities and fixed boundaries do not preclude cultural mixing. Ethnic variation may well exist without significant cultural variation. Therefore, processes of cultural mixing say little about group identities and degrees of boundedness.

Second: fluid identities, conversely, do not preclude cultural stability or continuity. Cultural variation can exist without ethnic variation or other kinds of strong group boundaries. Culture is an implication of varying degrees of shared meaning, while group identities result from clear, if disputed, social boundaries.

Third: the political usages of cultural symbols do preclude the people in question from having anything in common. Historiography, it has been shown time and again, is necessarily a selective and biased discipline simply because far too many events have taken place in the past for any historian to give all of them a fair treatment. Yet its slanted narratives may become self-fulfilling prophecies in that they give the readership (often schoolchildren) a shared frame of reference. Besides, the people described by nationalist historians or ideologists of group boundedness may not have that in common which their ideologists ascribe to them, but they may have other important cultural elements in common, such as shared jokes or ideas about kin relatedness. What has interested writers on cultural mixing are the situations where these frames of references do not function; where they are contested, non-existent or are being continuously rebuilt. But it may just happen to be the case, in other words, that ethnic boundaries coincide with certain cultural ones. (Moreover, the fact that something is socially constructed does not imply that it is unreal.)

This means that the ambiguous grey zones, which can be located to the space between categories and boundaries under pressure, are privileged sites for studying the interplay between culture and identity. This is not because all boundaries eventually disappear but because they are made visible through their negotiation and re-negotiation, transcendence, transformations and reframing.

I FORMS OF MIXING

There are a number of different outcomes from long-term encounters between distinct groups. Sometimes, one group is eventually absorbed into the other; sometimes it is absorbed culturally but not socially (the ethnic boundaries remain intact); sometimes the groups merge to create a new entity; sometimes a hierarchical complementary relationship or a symmetrical competitive relationship occurs; sometimes, again, one group eventually exterminates the other.

The anthropologist Olivia Harris (1995), writing on cultural complexity in Latin America and particularly the Andean area, has proposed a typology depicting six possible ways of conceptualizing long-term, regular contact between originally discrete groups.

First, she describes a model she simply calls *mixing*, in Latin America spoken of as *mestizaje*. This model shows how new meanings are generated from the mixing of diverse influences. This model corresponds to common usage of the terms hybridity and creolization.

The second model is the one of *colonization*, which in the South American context implies European dominance, exploitation and violence towards Indians, including the enforced introduction of Christianity and the Spanish language. This model is strongly dualist and somewhat mechanical in its notion of power and, in Harris's view, draws a rather too strict line between European and Indian culture, reifying ('freezing') both in the act. This may be true, but it remains a fact that the social boundaries (if not the cultural ones) between Indians and Europeans have remained largely intact, notwithstanding the emergence of intermediate categories such as the mestizo.

Third, an alternative to the rigid model of colonization implies the attribution of 'more agency to the colonized' and a phrasing of 'the relationship in terms of borrowing'. The traditions remain discrete, but Indian elites (Harris refers particularly to Incas and Mayas) borrow knowledge from the Christians. This is classic *diffusionism*.

The fourth model is 'that of juxtaposition or alternation, where two radically different knowledge systems are both accepted without a direct attempt at integration.' Since, for example, Maya and Christian cosmologies entailed fundamentally different conceptualizations of time and of the past, they could not be mixed, but actors could draw situationally on either. This is a variety of *multiculturalism*.

The fifth way of conceptualizing the meeting is 'that of imitation, assimilation or direct identification', whereby persons self-consciously reject their own past and adopt a self-identity and knowledge system they perceive as better or more beneficial to themselves. A conversion from Indian to mestizo identity in the Andes, Harris notes, 'usually involves wholesale rejection of Indian identity, in favour of and identification with what is seen as white or Hispanic.'

The sixth and final mode discussed by Harris is that of 'innovation and creativity', where 'attention is firmly removed from contrasted knowledge systems and priority is given to autonomy and independent agency.' Unlike the five other models sketched, this kind of conceptualization does not focus on origins.

All these models refer to mixing either at the level of identity, at the level of symbolic meaning or both, but they are clearly distinctive from one another. All can be used to make sense of contemporary encounters between different cultural systems.

Let us now look more closely at two of the most common concepts used to describe cultural mixing today.

2 HYBRIDITY AND CREOLIZATION

The concept of *cultural creolization*, owing its influence in anthropology to Ulf Hannerz (Hannerz 1992; but see also Drummond 1980), refers to the intermingling and mixing of two or several formerly discrete traditions or cultures. In an era of global mass communication and capitalism, creolization, according to this usage, can be identified nearly everywhere in the world, but there are important differences as to the degrees and forms of mixing. As mentioned above, this perspective has been criticized for essentializing cultures (as if the merging traditions were 'pure' at the outset, cf. Friedman 1994). Although this critique may sometimes be relevant, the concept nevertheless helps making sense of a great number of contemporary cultural processes, characterized by movement, change and fuzzy boundaries.

Creolization, as it is used by some anthropologists, is an analogy taken from linguistics. This discipline in turn took the term from a particular aspect of colonialism, namely the uprooting and displacement of large numbers of people in the plantation economies of certain colonies, such as Louisiana, Jamaica, Trinidad, Réunion and Mauritius. Both in the Caribbean basin and in the Indian Ocean, certain (or all) groups who contributed to this economy during slavery were described as creoles. Originally, a *criollo* meant a European (normally a Spaniard) born in the New World (as opposed to *peninsulares*); today, a similar usage is current in the French *département* La Réunion, where everybody born in the island, regardless of skin colour, is seen as *créole*, as opposed to the *zoreils* who were born in metropolitan France. In Trinidad, the term 'creole' is sometimes used to designate all Trinidadians except those of Asian origin. In Suriname, a 'creole' is a person of African origin, while in neighbouring French Guyana a 'creole' is a person who has adopted a European way of life. In spite of the differences, there are some important resemblances between the various conceptualizations of 'the creole', which resonate with the theoretical concept of creolization: 'creoles' are uprooted, they belong to the New World, are the products of some form of mixing, and are contrasted with that which is old, deep and rooted.

A question often posed by people unfamiliar with the varying uses of the term is: 'What is *really* a creole?' They may have encountered the term in connection with food or architecture from Louisiana, languages in the Caribbean or people in the Indian Ocean. Whereas vernacular uses of the term vary, there exist accurate definitions of creole languages in linguistics and of cultural creolization in anthropology. There are nevertheless similarities, although there is no one-to-one relationship between the ethnic groups described locally as creoles in particular societies, and the phenomena classified as creole or creolized in the academic literature.

Hybridity is a more general concept than creolization, and it may be used to refer to any obviously mixed cultural form. World music, various forms of contemporary 'crossover' cuisine and urban youth cultures borrowing elements from a variety of sources including minority cultures and TV, are typical examples of phenomena explored under the heading 'hybridity'.

Often, generic terms like creolization, hybridity or simply mixing may be adequate to describe cultural phenomena and processes resulting from the increased contact of globalization. Sometimes, more precision is needed, especially when cultural processes are connected with social ones.

Different parts of a cultural environment, and of people's life-worlds, are being affected by influence from outside at different speeds and to differing degrees. Sometimes people are acutely aware of changes taking place in their immediate environment, and take measures to stop it, to enhance it or to channel it in their preferred direction. At other times, people may be unaware of these processes, even if foreign influences and cultural mixing may change their cultural environment profoundly. These are some of the intricacies of contemporary cultural processes that need disentangling if we are to be successful in studying them accurately. Merely stating that mixing is an inherent feature of contemporary culture is no more enlightening than saying that cultural diffusion is a fact. Thus:

- *Cultural pluralism* directs the attention of the researcher towards the relative boundedness of the constituent groups or categories that make up a society. It is a close relative of multiculturalism.
- *Hybridity* directs attention towards individuals or cultural forms that are reflexively – self-consciously – mixed, that is syntheses of cultural forms or fragments of diverse origins. It opposes multiculturalism seen as 'nationalism writ small'.
- *Syncretism* directs attention towards the amalgamation of formerly discrete world views, cultural meaning and, in particular, religion.
- *Diasporic identity* directs attention towards an essentially social category consisting of people whose primary subjective belonging is in another country.
- *Transnationalism* directs attention, rather, to a social existence attaching individuals and groups not primarily to one particular place, but to several or none.
- *Diffusion* directs attention towards the flow of substances and meanings between societies, whether it is accompanied by actual social encounters or not.

■ *Creolization*, finally, directs our attention towards cultural phenomena which result from displacement and the ensuing social encounter and mutual influence between two or several groups, creating an ongoing dynamic interchange of symbols and practices, eventually leading to new forms with varying degrees of stability. The term *creole culture* suggests the presence of a standardized, relatively stable cultural idiom resulting from such a process. *Cultural decreolization* occurs when, in the case of group-based power differentials and inequalities, the subordinate group is socially or culturally assimilated into the dominant one (for example, *cholos* becoming *mestizos* in Latin America), or when a creolized idiom is 'purified' and made similar to a metropolitan or 'high culture' form (see Stewart 2007).

3 WORLD MUSIC

One of the most intensively studied areas of cultural mixing is that to do with music. Although music has, perhaps more easily than language, always been influenced by impulses from afar – Mozart's 'Turkish March' speaks for itself, Bártok's string quartets were influenced by Gypsy music, Grieg's 'Peer Gynt Suite' took elements from Scandinavian folk music – the most (in)famous contemporary example of cultural mixing in music is that of so-called world music: jazz musicians borrow from Indian ragas, rock musicians borrow from African percussive music, house and techno technicians borrow from the Javanese gamelan, and Jamaicans borrow from, and lend to, everybody. There are large-scale festivals devoted to world music (the oldest, and most famous, in Europe being Peter Gabriel's WOMAD festival); the genre (if it is a genre) has its own shelves in the music shops, its own labels and its own charts.

The term 'world music', as it has been established in everyday language since the late 1980s, testifies to an increased mobility of musicians, especially from the Third World, a greater intensity in the networks engaged in between musicians of diverse origin, and a faster flow of musical impulses across the globe. The mixed musical forms labelled world music are thus a prime example of intensified globalization.

In a critical assessment of the genre, entitled 'A lullaby for world music', the anthropologist and ethnomusicologist Steven Feld (2003: 195) describes how 'any and every hybrid or traditional style could ... be lumped together by the single market label *world music*', adding that this signified not only the triumph of the commercial but also a disquieting *banalization of difference*. The mixing represented in this kind of world music, as it is described by Feld, is a surprisingly close relative of the 'globalization of nothing' phenomenon analysed by Ritzer (cf. Chapter 4). However, Feld notes that this tendency is counteracted with a yearning for authenticity and the non-commercial. He also adds that the discourse about world music, academic and non-academic alike is, 'like globalization discourse more generally ... equally routed through the public sphere via tropes of anxiety and celebration' (Feld 2003: 198).

But the analysis does not stop there. Taking as an example a song, *Rorogwela*, composed by Afunakwa, a Baegu woman from the Solomon Islands, Feld goes on to show how oral and indigenous music is being transformed and re-created by Western musicians, and describes the difficulties involved in giving the original composers recognition and their rightful part of the revenues generated. In discussing this topic, Feld touches upon a much larger family of issues, namely those to do with intellectual property rights (IPRs). In an era where the cultural production of traditional peoples is being repackaged as commercially palatable 'exotic' products, it has become a question of key importance to many, especially indigenous peoples themselves, to be able to defend their legal rights to their music, literature and handicrafts (see Kasten 2004).

Contrasting a UNESCO series of authentic recordings of traditional music with the commercial adaptation of similar (sometimes identical) music, Feld ends his 'lullaby' with a remark about the way in which 'world music participates in shaping a kind of consumer-friendly multiculturalism, one that follows the market logic of expansion and consolidation' (Feld 2003: 213). Although many forms of musical mixing exist in our era of intensified globalization, and musicians from the Third World occasionally get their share of the profits and recognition, the commercial dimension of mixing – the world of Benetton – can rarely be disregarded altogether.

The flows of musical influences often have paradoxical effects. Lewellen (2002) describes the development of the Congolese rhumba from the 1920s to the 1940s, a guitar-based style borrowing from Cuban music. By the 1970s, the influence from soul was also apparent: partly African in origin, Cuban music and American soul returned to Africa, to be merged with locally developed styles. Later, a variant of Congolese popular music, the *soukouss*, became fashionable in Europe, where it was regarded as 'la vraie musique africaine'. However, *soukouss* was hardly listened to in Africa itself, where the lyrics sung in local languages, often strongly political, were as important as melody and rhythm.

4 A 'MIXED' FAMILY IN MAURITIUS

Writings on the globalization of culture tend to be full of anecdotes revealing the disembeddedness of cultural signs or connections between the local and the global, but it is also necessary to pay close attention to the wider implications of such processes at the level of everyday life. I shall now provide a brief example, a main purpose of which is to emphasize the continued relevance of anthropological fieldwork in a world where the small-scale work of ethnography may seem incapable of grasping the global forces at work.

Rose-Hill is a Mauritian town of some 40,000 inhabitants, according to statistics. However, boundaries between Mauritian towns are unclear, and it would probably be most accurate to describe Rose-Hill as one of five or six nodes along the nearly continuous urbanized stretch from Port-Louis to Curepipe, where about half of the ethnically diverse Mauritian population of a million lives.

The quarter of Roches-Brunes, located on the western outskirts of Rose-Hill, is dominated by a municipal housing estate (*cité ouvrière*), and most of the approximately 1,000 people living in the area are working-class Creoles or blacks.

Rushdie and Naipaul: Two Views on Mixing

Among the many novelists who have depicted the cultural complexities and dilemmas in postcolonial societies, V.S. Naipaul and Salman Rushdie are possibly the most famous in the English-speaking world. Naipaul, born in Trinidad in 1932, is the grandson of Indian immigrants and migrated to Britain in 1949, publishing novels, travel writing and essays since the mid-1950s. Among Naipaul's most celebrated books are *A House for Mr. Biswas* (1961) and *The Enigma of Arrival* (1987). Naipaul received the Nobel Prize for literature in 2001. Rushdie, born in Bombay (now Mumbai) on the eve of Indian independence in 1947, grew up in England and had a major breakthrough with *Midnight's Children*, an epic novel about the first years of Indian independence. In 1988, with the publication of the very complex and allegorical novel *The Satanic Verses*, Rushdie was accused of blasphemy against Islam, and the Iranian Ayatollah Khomeini proclaimed a *fatwa*, a death sentence on the writer.

Both Rushdie and Naipaul describe the intensive cultural mixing taking place both in postcolonial cities such as Bombay (Rushdie) and in the Caribbean (Naipaul), as well as through the migration experience. Interestingly, they seem to represent diametrically opposed views on cultural mixing, Rushdie being an optimist seeing the enriching and liberating power of 'mongrelization' as he once called it, while Naipaul is wary and deeply critical of what he sees as inauthentic mimicry and superficial cultural forms unable to anchor the individual in a strong tradition.

Naipaul's early, comic novels are satires of what he sees as Trinidadian vulgarity, the 'carnival mentality' where Trinidadians, in noisy and superficial ways, mix cultural impulses they have done nothing to deserve, in order to create an identity consisting of shiny surfaces with no intimation of depth or coherence. Members of an impure, hybrid creole culture, Trinidadians are mimicking metropolitan culture in Naipaul's view: In

The more imposing dwellings belonging to a few affluent families are located away from the more monotonous *cité ouvrière*. Apart from the Creoles, some coloureds (light-skinned Creoles with middle-class aspirations) and Chinese live in the area, as well as a few Hindus and a single Muslim household. Roches-Brunes is not representative of Mauritius with regards to ethnicity, as the largest 'community' islandwide is Hindu.

In describing the relationship between the global and the local, I shall focus on the Rioux household. It is what is commonly described as a matrifocal household, consisting of Mme Rioux, her daughter Aline (20), her two sons, François and Jean, both in their mid-twenties, Aline's baby daughter and a lodger, a young student from the neighbouring island of Rodrigues. Their income is average by local standards. Aline works as a shopgirl in the town centre, her elder brother François is a carpenter's apprentice, and her younger brother Jean is unemployed. The household sometimes

---

the late 1950s, he described how all the men leaving a cinema in Port-of-Spain after viewing *Casablanca* had immediately adopted Humphrey Bogart's style of walking. After *Biswas*, Naipaul's novels were increasingly melancholy, sometimes bitter depictions of thwarted or dishonest attempts at creating secure, firm identities. He is at his most cynical and devastating when he writes about Asian Muslims (in *Among the Believers*, 1981, and *Beyond Belief*, 1998) — converts, he calls them, even if, strictly speaking, they have been Muslims all their lives and can refer to centuries of Islamic faith in their countries.

Salman Rushdie has no time for cultural purism. 'A bit of this and a bit of that; that is how newness enters the world,' he writes in *Imaginary Homelands* (1991), in a celebration of the hybridization and cultural mixing caused by international migration, the global flows of ideas and the spread of a world-view which is open to change and ambivalent to tradition and inherited identities. In *Fury* (2001), Rushdie satirizes a postmodern identity movement in a lightly concealed version of Fiji, which dons clothes and code names from *Star Trek*; in *The Satanic Verses* (1988), arguably a literary masterpiece, he lashes out against all attempts to close the world and fix its boundaries, from orthodox religion to xenophobic nationalism. Even Rushdie's language, quite unlike Naipaul's economic, sober English, is exuberant and full of neologisms and expressions from Hindi and Indian English.

Naipaul and Rushdie exemplify two views of cultural purity and mixing, but also two views of creativity. Is it through mixing existing material in new ways, or through writing from a well defined vantagepoint embedded in a tradition, that human creativity is given the most fertile conditions? Such questions are characteristic of many debates about the globalization of culture, and they have several possible answers.

receives remittances from other relatives, notably a married daughter who lives in the neighbouring French *département*, La Réunion, and the student from Rodrigues pays a monthly rent.

The living-room in the Rioux' home contains several objects signifying links with distant places. Two posters depicting pop stars (one English, one American) are prominently displayed; so is a cupboard with glass doors, behind which are souvenirs from Paris, Bombay and London (gifts from foreigners). There is a radiocassette and a black-and-white TV set. On the floor next to the TV set, there is a small heap of foreign magazines, some of them in English, which is a language none of the household member masters. Images of Europe are powerful and persuasive in Mauritius; an opinion poll carried out in the mid-1970s indicated that half of the population wished to emigrate if they could (see Eriksen 1998).

The mass media consumed in the household confirm the common stereotype of life in 'the Western world' as an easy, glamorous life. Local knowledge of Europe generally suggests it is a continent of affluence and excitement. Many Mauritians have emigrated, the majority to France and Britain. Aline Rioux says she wouldn't emigrate; she has heard too many ugly stories of girls who were forced into prostitution, or who were married to old men living in the countryside. There has, in other words, been a certain feedback from other parts of the global system. She reads *romans-photo*, 'photo-novels' of French origin, and occasionally a local magazine. She is fond of French pop music.

François Rioux plays soccer and follows world politics in the local newspapers; he frequently discusses global issues with his friends. The whole family watches American soap operas on TV; the younger generation go to the cinema to see largely American films dubbed in French about twice a month. They are devoted Catholics and go to Mass every Sunday (actually, Aline goes somewhat more rarely).

The members of the household agree that education is important for a person's opportunities, unless he or she has relatives in high places. François, Jean and Aline are all prepared to compete for jobs and promotion. None of them have completed secondary school.

Seen superficially and in a fragmented way, the world-structures and patterns of consumption of the Rioux household seem comparable to, similar to, that of working classes in many other countries. The globalization of culture seems predominant in Roches-Brunes, which to an untrained observer like the Lévi-Strauss of *Tristes Tropiques* (1955), must seem a squalid backyard of civilization. Scrutinized more closely, however, the lives and world-structures of the Rioux and the others in the *cité* have a distinctively local character, and cannot at all be understood outside of their local context.

Football and pop music may credibly be seen as prime instances of global culture. Football in Roches-Brunes follows the same rules as in Britain. Unlike World Cup football, however, it is entirely local in character. François Rioux owes much of his reputation in the neighbourhood to his skills as a football player. As a result, he is popular with the girls, makes friends with the boys and in fact, he got his present job at least partly because of his personal popularity. Concerning pop music, so arrogantly despised by most anthropologists who encounter it in the field, a similar local context applies. It is played at local parties and in rumshops, and may evoke sentiments and stimulate social relations quite different from its effects in other environments. In the black Jamaican working-class, for example, the world-famous pop singer Michael Jackson was controversial already in the late 1980s because he was considered 'not sufficiently black'; in the black Mauritian working class he is second only to God, not least because he is considered black.

When watching American TV serials (dubbed in French), the Rioux comment on them incessantly. Very often, they compare the characters with people they know; when commenting on rich and miserly men, they might make remarks to the effect that 'Hey, that's just like Lee Foo used to treat my friend', referring to a neighbourhood Chinese merchant. They always compare the plots and social milieux on the screen with contexts they are familiar with. It should also be noted, significantly, that for a Mauritian Creole, European culture is attractive partly because it is reflexively being contrasted locally with Mauritian Hindu culture. Films and magazines describing middle-class life in Europe or North America, for example, thus make sense and are popular partly because they can be interpreted into a local dichotomous schema depicting Indian culture as inferior. Overcommunicating what is locally perceived as Europeanness indicates a culturally valued air of superiority compared with the local Indians. In their selective interpretations of aspects of global culture, the inhabitants of Roches-Brunes appropriate them and transform the global into something local.

There are sound reasons why the thesis of globalization, in its most general and sweeping forms, should be treated with great caution. For one thing, local life-worlds are produced and reproduced locally, and there are social fields where the globalization of culture has little or no effect – for example in the socialization of children, where Mauritian Creole custom is strikingly different from that of the hegemonic white Franco-Mauritians. For another, there are large parts of the world where the globalizing agencies hardly enter. *Poverty*, it needs to be mentioned, functions as an efficient anti-globalization mechanism in these matters. The very poor have scant access to the shared interfaces of modernity, nor are the agencies of modernity particularly interested in providing them.

5 A MODEL

The politics of identity, this chapter has suggested, is interwoven with cultural mixing in complex ways. There is no one-to-one relationship between cultural mixing and political cosmopolitanism or tolerance, nor can it be assumed that a yearning for cultural purity necessarily goes together with a xenophobic or nationalist political attitude. However, as will be made clear in Chapter 8, an ideology of cultural purity very often accompanies an identity politics that stresses the virtues of the in-group and, by implication, stereotypes outsiders.

Let us consider some possible options for people living in societies exposed to a variety of cultural influences, both from the inside and from outside – in a word, fairly typical societies in our present age.

At the ideological level, some promote mixing, whereas others are favourable to purity. At the level of social integration, some emphasize the need for similarity within a given society, while others are happy to accept considerable diversity or difference. These dimensions can be combined in altogether four ways (see Figure 6.1).

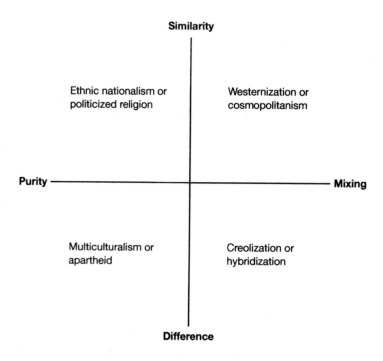

Figure 6.1. Some possible positions in discourses about culture and identity (from Eriksen 2007b)

Cultural purity and similarity are championed by nationalism and politicized religion. The outside world is seen as a source of contamination.

Mixing and similarity would typically be defended by groups and persons who either see Westernization as a good thing (associated with progress, education and so forth) or who argue that society ought to rest on the shared values of cosmopolitanism, the view that differences must exist but they must be tolerated, and dialogue across cultural divides bring people more closely together.

An emphasis on purity along with an acceptance of differences within society seems to be a recipe for segregation. South African apartheid is an obvious example, but there are also forms of multiculturalism in the contemporary north Atlantic world that fit this description: Different groups, with different values and customs, should co-exist without enforced contact or missionary activity.

Finally, a favourable attitude towards both mixing and difference sets the stage for a society where hybridity or, in societies like Mauritius, creolization is considered unproblematic and virtuous. The absence of clear boundaries is not seen as a problem and the emphasis is on the individual's freedom to adapt or adopt the values and practices he or she deems valuable.

The four corners of the figure are not mutually exclusive in practice (the real world tends to muddy neat models). In most societies, these options co-exist, often in conflicting ways, sometimes in precarious equilibria. In many coastal hamlets in northern Norway, where there has been a recent revitalization of Sami (Lappish) identity, families are split over which identity to choose. These families are of mixed origins, and were for generations subjected to a policy of 'Norwegianization', as a result of which many consider themselves Norwegian and not Sami. When some family members choose to return to the Sami identity of (some of) their ancestors and others refuse to have anything to do with Sami culture or identity, one can only imagine the silences during Sunday dinner. It could moreover be argued that the 1990s wars in Yugoslavia were, at the ideological level, fought between a model of ethnic nationalism and a model of cosmopolitanism or multiculturalism. Less violently, but seriously enough, French language policy has in recent decades sought to purge French of English loanwords, at the same time as the descendants of Arab immigrants devise their own forms of hybrid French influenced by Arab and Berber syntax and vocabulary.

Mixing is usually controversial but it takes place continuously. A task for researchers is to discover and analyse the forms of mixing not commented upon, those that are endorsed and those which are actively resisted or fought over. Every society has its own peculiar debates about cultural mixing, and one of their elements is always globalization.

Chapter Summary

- The cultural mixing resulting from globalization takes many forms, usually indicating power discrepancies between the groups involved.
- Mixing at the cultural level does not preclude strengthened group identification.
- Cultural mixing does not create homogeneity, but new configurations of diversity.
- An important objection against theories of hybridity and creolization is that cultures have never been pure and bounded.
- The cultural diffusion associated with globalization cannot simply be described as 'Westernization', but usually is better depicted as a form of cultural glocalization.

7 VULNERABILITY

We joined Europe to have free movement of goods ... I did not join Europe to have free movement of terrorists, criminals, drugs, plant and animal diseases and rabies and illegal immigrants.

Margaret Thatcher

INTRODUCTION

The terrorist attacks on 11 September 2001 signalled a new phase in the public awareness of what globalization was about. The upbeat optimism of the 1990s, when globalization was above all associated with the Internet, political freedom, individualism and democracy among intellectuals and the general public alike was suddenly replaced by a heightened awareness of globalization as a volatile, anarchic and dangerous state: it signalled the loss of control. While freedom, seen as an individual right, had been the main template for globalization in the 1990s, its close relative, insecurity, now came to the forefront.

Although people may in a traditional past have been no more secure in their lives than we are – in many cases they were far less secure – at least they tended to belong to a community by default. Nobody challenged their group membership, whether it was based on kin, religion or locality; they knew who to turn to in times of need and scarcity, and they had a clear notion of the moral universe within which they lived. When contemporary social theorists speak of our era as somehow more insecure than the past, this is roughly what they tend to have in mind. Zygmunt Bauman's concept *liquid modernity* (Bauman 2000) concerns the floating, shifting qualities of values and social structure in our era; Ulrich Beck's *risk society* (Beck 1992 [1986]) refers not to increased objective risks, but a heightened awareness of risks; and Anthony Giddens's term *post-traditional society* (Giddens 1991) describes a society where a tradition can no longer be taken for granted, but must actively be defended *vis-à-vis* its alternatives, which now appear realistic.

These and many other concepts used to describe an era of increased inter-connectedness suggest that globalization makes people more vulnerable because the conditions for their existence are no longer locally produced and cannot be controlled.

Climate change, AIDS, terrorism, avian influenza and SARS: there is a wide-spread feeling of vulnerability, easily translatable into a subjective sense of insecurity and powerlessness, in an era where conditions for local life are often felt to be defined elsewhere, at an abstract 'global' level.

A term often preferred to 'vulnerability' is 'risk'. Risk can be defined as a function of probability and consequences. If the probability is high and the consequences negligible, the risk is estimated to be low. Conversely, even if the probability is minimal, the risk is considered high if the consequences are enormous. Of course, it is rarely possible to estimate risk objectively, but risk assessment is still important and can trigger action·in many widely different areas, from financial investment to climate change.

As Ulrich Beck writes, risks are in a sense both real and unreal: some risks have visible consequences already today (from terrorist attacks to deaths caused by water pollution), but 'on the other hand, the actual social impetus of risks lies in the *projected dangers of the future*' (Beck 1992: 34). Beck's seminal *Risk Society*, and many later books on risk, are concerned with issues like environmental destruction and climate change, AIDS and other transnational diseases, terrorism and deterritorialized conflicts. Although Beck's original statement was concerned with what he saw as a transformation of modernity, towards a less self-confident, less secure situation, the insights from the sociology of risk can easily be transposed to the transnational canvas.

I NATURAL AND MANUFACTURED RISKS?

Sometimes, a distinction is made between *natural* and *manufactured* risks (see, for example, Giddens 1999). Natural risks include snakebite and shark attacks, tsunamis and earthquakes, while the manufactured ones might have been avoided with the proper use of the foresight entailed by 'the precautionary principle', a notion that is widespread in the transnational environmentalist movement. However important it may be to indicate which risks and dangers can be avoided by human agency, there can be no sharp distinction between the two. If one knows the whereabouts of sharks, being attacked is not a purely natural event if one chooses to go into the water.

A more complex and more interesting example is that of the tsunami that struck coastal areas in several Asian countries on Boxing Day, 2004. Many thousand were killed, mostly locals, but a considerable number of tourists also perished. The material damage was enormous in Thailand, Malaysia and Indonesia. In an important sense, the tsunami was a natural accident. The cause was an underwater volcanic eruption; it had nothing to do with the depletion of fish stocks, global warming or pollution. At the same time, it was argued that with proper precautionary measures, such as an efficient early warning system, much of the damage could have been avoided.

There is an interesting parallel between the tsunami and the Lisbon earthquake in 1755. The latter was seen all over Europe as a horrible disaster. Some believed it was caused by the wrath of God; others saw it as an example of the amorality of nature and the lack of a higher meaning; yet others argued that the consequences were partly a result of poor foresight. Rousseau, in particular, argued that if the Portuguese had been less urbanized and lived in a different kind of housing, the number of casualties would have been much lower. Voltaire, on the contrary, saw the earthquake as a meaningless event signifying the death of God and the futility of an overly optimistic belief in progress. Rousseau, thus, represented the voice of those who called for proper early warning systems in 2004.

By an uncanny coincidence, a major academic book on risk and vulnerability (Wisner et al. 2004), published on the eve of the South-East Asian tsunami, uses a Japanese painting of a tsunami as its cover image. Ben Wisner and his co-authors there make a powerful argument against the idea that certain forms of vulnerability, or risk, are purely natural while others are manufactured. Following a similar line of argument to Rousseau, they argue that urbanization has led to a great increase in vulnerability in the poor parts of the world. The high population densities of cities makes it easy for disease to spread and settlers in urban areas often have no other option than to 'occupy unsafe land, construct unsafe habitations or work in unsafe environments' (Wisner et al. 2004: 70).

Although many risks and vulnerabilities are produced locally and can be alleviated through domestic policies, there can be no doubt that many different forms of vulnerability have been globalized, the most obvious being those that affect the poorest. Structural adjustments, aiming to improve the economic performance of Third World countries, have led to cuts in public expenditure on health and education, and have led to large-scale unemployment in many countries. The rich North Atlantic countries continue to protect their own agricultural sectors through subsidies and import tariffs, while encouraging poor countries to 'open up' their economies. Dependence on export earnings, typical of many Third World agricultural sectors, increases vulnerability because reliance on one or a few products reduces flexibility. If the cocoa crop fails or the price of cocoa declines, the consequences for the Ivorian economy are very serious indeed. In a past when agricultural production was largely for the local market or even the domestic sphere (the household), agriculture was more diverse and better able to withstand temporary setbacks affecting one or a few crops.

Although droughts and floods are natural occurrences (which may nonetheless be linked to global climate change), their consequences are anything but natural, and the causes of those consequences may often be traced to transnational economics (enhancing vulnerability) and the world of development aid (preventing some of the most horrible consequences). Thus, Rousseau was right in his unwillingness to blame disasters on God or nature alone. Even natural hazards are to some extent socially manufactured.

The AIDS epidemic and globalization

Epidemic diseases have played a major part in human history, not least in periods when there has been large-scale contact between formerly mutually isolated groups (McNeill 1976; Diamond 1998). Diseases that were trivial to Europeans, who had lived in close contact with domestic animals for millennia, were deadly to many native Americans.

The AIDS epidemic is deadly everywhere, but its consequences vary geographically. Believed to have originated in central Africa, AIDS was first diagnosed in a group of homosexual men in Los Angeles in 1981. Soon found to exist in the Caribbean (Haiti) as well, AIDS had been reported in 85 countries by the end of 1986. Today, it is estimated that 70,000 to 100,000 persons had been infected with the disease before it was named.

Since the mid-1980s, AIDS has spread quickly, but unevenly, throughout the world. In the North Atlantic, it remains a disease associated with syringe users and homosexual men. In the Middle East and North Africa, it is a rare disease, clearly due to strong cultural restrictions on extramarital sex. In certain parts of Asia, notably India, China and some south-east Asian countries like Thailand, the disease is spreading quickly. Finally, in many countries in sub-Saharan Africa, the social and economic consequences of AIDS are, and have for some years been, disastrous. By 2006, eleven countries in this region had lost more than a tenth of their labour force because of AIDS.

The uneven spread of AIDS illustrates a general fact about globalization: ideas, things and people move faster than before, but not indiscriminately. Factors affecting their uneven movement are cultural, economic and political. Yet it must be pointed out that in a non-globalized world or even in a slower, globalized world, the AIDS epidemic would have spread much more slowly if at all.

2 PERCEIVED RISK AND REAL CONSEQUENCES

Perceived vulnerability has increased in the rich countries too. The complexity of global systems precludes a proper overview and makes it difficult to make decisions on the basis of sound knowledge. The extent of a given risk or danger is difficult to estimate. Most of the readers will have vivid memories of the global anthrax scare in the autumn of 2001. Appearing just after the 9/11 terrorist attacks, the appearance of deadly anthrax spores in letters sent to a few individuals on the US east coast was widely believed to be an alternative form of terrorism and many believed that the al-Qaeda terrorist network was behind it.

The varying impact of the AIDS epidemic also shows how vulnerability is contingent on many factors. In the rich northern countries, antiretroviral drugs now make it possible to live with HIV for many years without contracting AIDS. In most Muslim countries, transmission of the disease is slow and inefficient for cultural reasons. In Thailand and India, prostitutes are a main source of transmission, whereas the pattern is different in many African countries, where casual sex is common and women account for roughly half of the infected. In Botswana, Lesotho, Swaziland and Zimbabwe, the adult HIV prevalence rate is over 20 per cent. Life expectancy has plunged. Millions of children are orphaned. Economic growth is set back. Some African politicians even deny that AIDS is caused by HIV.

However, some African countries have been successful in containing AIDS, notably Uganda, where the prevalence has fallen from 15 per cent in the early 1990s to around 5 per cent in 2005. The general explanation is that the Ugandan state, supported by international NGOs, has successfully taught the population how to avoid being infected. The condom, although opposed by powerful transnational actors like the Catholic Church, has been a key object in this respect. The antiretroviral drugs that prevent HIV from developing into AIDS are expensive, and transnational lawsuits are fought over the right to develop cheaper generic drugs for the benefit of Africans and others in poorer countries.

The HIV/AIDS epidemic illustrates the interwoven character of the contemporary world. It spread and grew thanks to the increased mobility of people, it has varying consequences locally because of important cultural, economic and political differences between countries, and it can only be fought efficiently through transnational co-operation.

Less than a dozen received letters contained anthrax spores, all of them on the American east coast. Yet, the perceived risk of being killed by a seemingly innocent white powder lacing a letter was huge worldwide. Postal servicemen were instructed to treat suspicious letters and packages with particular caution, and commentators in the media feared that the world had only seen the beginning of a large-scale campaign. Many of those who did not believe in the al-Qaeda hypothesis speculated that an Iraqi scientist (she was named, her picture published in newspapers worldwide) was behind the campaign.

Interestingly, although no letters containing anthrax spores were found outside the US, where seventeen persons were infected and five died, heightened security surrounding mail deliveries was imposed in many countries. Thousands of false alarms led to the careful opening, by authorized personnel wearing airtight uniforms, of letters and packages worldwide. In a few cases, entire office buildings were evacuated where suspicious letters had been identified.

Although the anthrax crime has, at the time of writing, not been solved, it has been ruled out that the letters had anything to do with either Iraq or the al-Qaeda.

The example nicely sums up the argument so far: Perceived risk is a result of anticipated consequences rather than 'scientific' probability; contemporary risks travel easily across and between continents; and there are enormous uncertainties involved in risk assessment. The fact that many risks are proven to be much less significant than commonly believed – what we fear is rarely that which kills us – the sociologist Frank Furedi (2002) has spoken of the contemporary obsession with risk as 'a culture of fear'. His argument is that the benefits from genetically modified foods, genetic research and mobile phones, to mention three of his examples, are much greater than the risks involved, and that policy should therefore be based on optimism rather than anxiety. This rejoinder from a colleague of Giddens, Beck and Bauman – three leading theorists who speak gravely of increased risk – should be kept in mind throughout this chapter. Since risks are largely psychological, their relationship to reality can always be disputed. It is nevertheless difficult to dispute the fact that some of the key issues of global politics at the early twenty-first century are to do with vulnerability and risk, both in rich and poor countries, although in different ways. Two of them, which we will discuss in some detail, are climate change and transnational terrorism.

3 CLIMATE CHANGE

When asked to illustrate what they mean by 'irreducible complexity', theorists sometimes evoke two examples of systems which are complex in such a way that they cannot be described properly in a simplified manner: The fluctuations in the global financial market, and the global climate. It comes as no surprise, therefore, that geophysicists and other climate experts disagree about the causes, likely effects and indeed the reality of contemporary climate change. Indeed, the US government failed to ratify the 2002 Kyoto protocol, an attempt to commit all countries to reduce their CO_2 emissions, ostensibly because its representatives did not trust the scientific findings underpinning the treaty.

This much said, the vast majority of experts are now convinced that the Earth's climate is changing, and that human activity – notably the massive emission of 'greenhouse gases' from industry, private appliances and traffic – is a main cause. The famous biologist James Lovelock, originator of the 'Gaia hypothesis' according to which the planet can be studied as a self-regulating organism, has compared the present situation to 'a fever'. In his 2006 book *The Revenge of Gaia*, Lovelock describes the narrow limits within which crucial parameters need to be for the Earth to be a livable place for a great variety of plants and animals. If the temperature increases with 5°C, the entire tropical belt becomes desert. If the proportion of oxygen in the atmosphere rises to 21 per cent a mere spark will lead to a fire, but if it declines to 15 per cent, it becomes impossible to light a fire.

Lovelock's book, which shows how icebergs and glaciers shrink, how deserts grow and the development of the global temperature of the last one hundred years can be mapped on a graph resembling a hockey stick, expresses an alarmist sense of vulnerability. With a population of a billion around 1800, he seems to argue, humanity could have done pretty much what we wanted; it would not have inflicted permanent damage on the precarious ecological equilibria of the planet. With a global population of over six billion (and growing), and a widespread technology based on fossil fuels, irreversible consequences are bound to occur.

A fascinating aspect of climate change is the way in which small changes may lead to enormous consequences, often on a global scale. In this way, climate change illustrates, better than most other global phenomena, the butterfly effect. Let us consider one brief example.

If the sea temperature in the tropical Pacific rises only a degree above the average, it results in the phenomenon known as El Niño in South America, leading to flooding in Peru and drought in Australia. As far away as the Amazon basin, the effects of El Niño are felt through dry and hot weather, which may last for months. Forest fires are likely in Indonesia. Along the west coast of South America, fish becomes less abundant because of the higher water temperatures and this, in turn, leads to a decrease in the guano production (fertilizer based on bird droppings). El Niño events also affect coral reefs adversely. During the 1997–8 El Niño, the enormous rainforest fires in Indonesia fed particles and smog into the ocean west of Sumatra. After the fires, the coastal seawater appeared to turn red, an effect caused by the proliferation of a tiny organism living off the iron in the smog particles. However, these organisms (dinoflagellates) produce toxins that kill coral organisms. Flannery (2006: 107) comments that 'it will take the reefs decades to recover, if indeed they ever do.'

El Niño (and El Niña, which is caused by cooling and has different consequences) has been a regularly recurring phenomenon for ever but many scientists believe that El Niño-like events are now becoming more common because of the overall effects of human-induced global warming.

4 CLIMATE CHANGE AND GLOBAL DEMOCRACY

Farmers in western Greenland, who grow potatoes and cereals, rejoice in their increased yields (Traufetter 2006). Summers have become perceptibly longer and warmer in the Arctic area over the last few decades. As a rule, under conditions of global warming, temperatures rise fastest near the poles. However, as is well known, the warmer conditions in Greenland entail warmer conditions elsewhere as well. Only a few degrees separate the Mediterranean from a semi-desert state, and when glaciers melt in the Arctic, the influx of freshwater into the North Atlantic is believed to have adverse consequences for the Gulf Stream. Consisting of salt water, heavier than the freshwater of the shrinking glaciers, the Gulf Stream may already have been considerably weakened. However, there have so far been no perceptible consequences for the temperatures of north-western Europe. Some scientists now argue that the contribution of ocean currents to climate have been exaggerated, and that wind systems are more important. Others point out that when the Gulf Stream has slowed in earlier periods, the temperature has dropped by as much as 10ºC in a decade.

The term 'environmental refugee' has occasionally been used in recent years to describe displaced persons fleeing an environment destroyed by human activity. Used in a wide sense, the term might encompass many of the world's slum dwellers – ex-farmers whose fields were destroyed by highways, ex-fishermen facing dwindling returns because of water pollution, and so on. More dramatic are stories about entire communities that have been displaced because of recurrent flooding or the thawing of the permafrost on which their villages were built.

In 2004, Inuit organizations appealed to the Inter-American Commission on Human Rights for a legal ruling concerning alleged damages to their livelihood caused by climate change. There has been a sharp decline in the numbers of the animals traditionally hunted by the Inuits (bear, seal, caribou), and villages are becoming uninhabitable because of thaw (Flannery 2006). On the other side of the Bering Straits and in northern Scandinavia, indigenous reindeer herders are facing serious problems because of recurrent mild periods in winter. Reindeer survive in winter by digging through the snow for lichen but melted snow becomes solid ice when refrozen. It cannot be dug through, and the animals frequently suffer fractures when they slip and fall.

The committee appealed to by the Inuits has no legal powers, but its ruling could make it possible to sue either the US government or US corporations. One can only imagine the complexities involved in suing transnational corporations for damages inflicted over perhaps a century, and contributing to climate change with locally harmful consequences.

In some ways, the consequences of climate change illustrate George Monbiot's (2003) view, that 'everything has been globalized except democracy'. It is difficult to see any international body, or organization, taking full responsibility for an entire nation forced to flee because of rising seawaters. Several Pacific states, along with the Maldives in the Indian Ocean, are flat coral atolls that would be wiped out if the water were to rise a couple of metres.

Things can even get much worse, as Lovelock, Flannery and many others are wont to point out. Many of the world's greatest cities, from Hong Kong to Calcutta and London are located on flat landscapes at sea level. Some, among them Lovelock, even believe that it is by now too late to reverse the tendency towards global warming and climatic instability. The world 'thermostat' is sluggish and has taken a severe beating to be brought onto the present course, they argue, and even with a dramatic reduction in greenhouse gas emissions, the turmoil continues.

5 RELIANCE ON EXPERT SYSTEMS

A minority of climatologists have argued that the main cause of current climatic instability is the high solar spot activity that has been noticed in recent years. Non-specialists, that is the vast majority of people, can only trust their own intuitions and what they are told by the experts when they make up their minds. Faced with expert systems of knowledge, trust is essential, but when experts disagree or are proven wrong, that trust begins to erode. This is a central argument in Beck's sociology of modernity (1992, 1999) and in Giddens' writings on 'late modernity' (1990, 1991), while Furedi (2002) has argued that the experts – scientific and technological – have in fact been right much more often than not.

132 globalization: the key concepts

The fact nevertheless remains that a strong reliance on the pronouncements of experts, which feed into policies, depends on widespread trust to be efficient, and that environmental issues have to some extent jeopardized the trusting relationship between experts and the public. The expert system, one of Giddens' main forms of disembedding (discussed in Chapter 1), is an abstract and arcane body of knowledge that is inaccessible to the vast majority of people.

Experts are sometimes wrong. Financial experts have been unable to predict stock market crashes. The strategic experts of the FBI and the CIA were unable to predict and prevent the terrorist attack on the USA in 2001. Experts on marine life disagree about the numbers of minke whales in the North Atlantic. Few if any experts on Eastern Europe were able to predict the rapid demise of Soviet-style communism and nobody predicted, in 1991, that Fidel Castro would still be in power in Cuba in 2007. Predictions about the spread of contagious diseases such as HIV-AIDS, SARS, Ebola and avian influenza (bird flu) vary wildly.

In the world of computers and fast information networks, even some of the major predictions have been proved wrong. In 1943, the IBM CEO Thomas Watson pronounced that there might be a world market for about five computers. In the early 1980s, when personal computers became common, pundits predicted the advent of the paperless office. A decade later, as advanced telecommunications made video conferences and telephone meetings possible and affordable, many predicted that this would reduce air travel. Finally, at the end of the twentieth century, there was global anxiety around the so-called Y2K issue (the 'millennium bug'), and billions were spent in attempting to prevent disaster.

The issue consisted in the fact that most of the world's mainframe computers, which ran lifts, ATMs, greenhouse thermostats, traffic lights, airspace controlling systems and so on, had their basic programming done in the 1960s and early 1970s, when bytes were expensive. For this reason, programmers skipped the first two digits of the year, typing '79' rather than '1979'. Because of the ambiguities arising on 1 January 2000, it was widely believed that computers worldwide would refuse to co-operate and break down. Even microcomputers like the one I am using now were believed to be 'at risk' because their software contained traces of the old software from the era before the cheap gigabyte.

Belief in Y2K overshadowed all other concerns associated with the turn of the millennium in the most computerized (richest) countries. Experts went on television stating that they had filled their basement with tinned food and water containers, their garage with firewood. Retired programmers were taken out of retirement to help re-programming the software. India's IT sector took off partly (some would say largely) because of the massive demand for programming expertise in the last couple of years of the twentieth century.

In the event, as everyone will recall, nothing dramatic happened to the world's computer driven systems as the century grinded to a halt, although it was reported that some Australian bus-ticket validation machines failed to operate after the turn of the millennium.

The faith placed in the reality of the Y2K problem by governments, enterprises and individuals all over the world suggests that the belief in expert systems can sometimes be regarded as blind faith. Lacking criteria for evaluating the predictions, many invoked the precautionary principle.

In a more serious vein, it should be noted that the expert knowledge systems used by transnational financial institutions such as the World Bank and the International Monetary Fund (IMF) have demonstrably failed to create economic stability and prosperity in the Third World countries that followed them (Gray 1998, Stiglitz 2002, Scholte 2005 and many others have documented this).

The feeling that one 'cannot even trust the experts', more pronounced in the rich countries than elsewhere, since the demotic political discourse in these countries presupposes that experts are to be trusted, has led many to abandon faith in technological progress and social engineering. Some have turned to religion, thereby falsifying the 'secularization thesis' popular among twentieth century sociologists, according to which rationalization would slowly erode the basis for religion. On the contrary, demand for religious meaning seems to be rising. In addition to many other things, religion can alleviate a sense of insecurity and meaninglessness. The revival of religion in the wake of partial or failed modernization is a global – and globalized – trend. Islam has become the main identity marker for many, if not most, Muslims in the world. Pentecostal missions across the world, often surprisingly co-ordinated in their activities, enjoy substantial success in countries as diverse as Ghana, the Philippines and Brazil. 'New Age' religions, that is eclectic mixtures of a variety of religious impulses, have many followers in the rich world. Through a curious recursive movement, new age religion, much of which had its origins in India but was 'Westernized' and adapted to modern society and lifestyles in the US, has enjoyed a recent popularity in India itself. (Rhythmic music has made a similar cyclical movement from Africa to the New World and back.)

Religion, generally poorly understood by the secularized academic elites, is a widespread alternative to the confusion, uncertainty and sense of vulnerability created by faltering expert systems in a world of fast movement, deterritorialization and change. It offers a coherent world and a meaning of life, usually including a mission in life, which has become increasingly difficult to deliver by the prophets of modernity.

6 GLOBALIZATION AND 'THE WAR ON TERROR'

To what extent the 9/11 terrorists were ultimately motivated by religious sentiment is debated, but it is a well documented fact that politicized religion has come to the forefront in many parts of the world in recent decades. The first example that comes to most readers' mind is that of political Islam, but political Hinduism has played a central role in Indian politics since the mid-1980s, and Christian interest groups have enjoyed growing influence on politics in the US. On a smaller scale, the number of witchcraft accusations has grown rapidly in many parts of Africa in recent years.

This is not the place to give a thorough treatment to religion in globalization (see Beyer 2006), but the religious element in the current 'war on terror', seen as a *jihad* against Jews and crusaders by the adversaries of the Western powers, is clearly very important, probably on both sides. In the present context, the emphasis is on the effects of deterritorialized warfare on perceived vulnerability.

The terrorist attacks that destroyed the World Trade Center and damaged the Pentagon on the morning of 11 September 2001 were difficult to classify using conventional criteria. The American president would soon denounce them with a declaration of 'war on terrorism', but as mentioned in an earlier chapter, war is normally declared on another country, not on an ideology or a deterritorialized political practice. The uncertainty concerning whether to see the terrorist acts as a very large crime or as a military attack implied a threat to the boundary between the outside and the inside of American society (Eriksen 2001b). Had it been interpreted as a crime, the federal police would have been charged with finding the surviving terrorists, collaborating with police elsewhere through the transnational police organization Interpol, involving intelligence personnel (spies in everyday language) when necessary. Since the government interpreted the attack as military, however, military retribution would be required. A temporary result of this interpretation was the presence of heavily armed soldiers at the entrances of public transport hubs such as the Grand Central Station in New York.

Enemies of a sovereign state are usually abroad, and could traditionally be identified as other states. However, these enemies seemed to be neither outside nor inside. Unlike terrorists in other locations, they were not just opposed to the political regime of the state but its very existence **and** that of its inhabitants (according to a declaration made by Osama bin Laden in 1998).

Some of the state's enemies were physically inside it. The suicide bombers were themselves *bona fide* residents of the US, several of them – infamously – students at a flight school (but curiously uninterested in learning how to land a plane).

However, the network of militant Islamists of which they were a part, al-Qaeda, was decentralized and to a great extent deterritorialized. This meant that the enemy was neither a group of insurgents or revolutionaries wishing to overthrow the regime in Washington, nor a resentful alien state.

As is well known, the reactions of the US to the terrorist attack were comprehensive and wide-ranging. A war was waged against the Taliban regime of Afghanistan, which had sheltered and supported al-Qaeda, and many of their leading officers were believed to hide in the country. With the Taliban removed from power in Kabul (and left to fight a perpetual guerrilla war against what they see as a puppet regime installed by the Americans), the US went to war against Iraq in 2003, following undocumented (and later disproved) claims that Iraq's secular dictator Saddam Hussein had a positive relationship with the al-Qaeda and that the country had developed 'weapons of mass destruction'. Years after the declaration of the 'war on terror', Osama bin Laden has (summer 2007) not yet been caught.

In the same period, in the words of human rights scholar Richard A. Wilson (2005), 'the Bush Administration advanced a formulation of international security that detached [human] rights from security concerns' (Wilson 2005: 6). The prison camp in the American Guantánamo base in Cuba, for example, is operated outside, and in violation of, international law. The US has also tried to undermine 'the ICC [International Criminal Court] through bilateral agreements which grant a special exemption from prosecution for US soldiers' (Wilson 2005: 6). Enhancing all forms of security associated with civilian air travel, the US has also fortified embassies overseas, sometimes moving them from city centres into locations easier to guard. The impression given to the outside world is that of a society under siege at home and at war abroad.

The failure of the US to destroy the al-Qaeda and associated groups illustrates a contrast introduced early in this book between the territorial power and the decentralized network. Any number of fighter planes, commandos and warheads is insufficient to destroy a versatile, flexible and mobile network of committed adversaries. At a structural level, the 'war on terror' has some resemblance to the attempts to remove child pornography from the Internet. States deploy their territorial power and may be able to find and catch users and some producers of child pornography but because the actual material is located on servers overseas, which can be moved quickly and easily to new locations, the offending pornography as such can scarcely be removed.

A survey commissioned by *Foreign Policy* in September 2006 indicated that 86 of the 100 experts surveyed believed that the world was now more dangerous than it was five years earlier, and 84 believed that the US was losing the war on terror. A significant majority believed that the country was becoming less safe as a result of the draconian measures, unpopular in large parts of the world, Muslim and non-Muslim, taken against terrorism.

The 'war on terror' is instructive as a lesson on globalization. First, it shows that the boundary between a society's inside and outside are relative. Second, it confirms the hypothesis that, in a global information society, flexible networks are a superior mode of organization to the territorially based hierarchy.

Third, it is an example of a truly transnational, deterritorialized conflict. Terrorist suspects (and perpetrators) have been caught in Spain, France, Denmark, Germany, Pakistan and many other countries.

Fourth, it gives many examples of the global repercussions of transnational processes. In the remote north Norwegian port of Tromsø, for example, an unbeautiful fence has been built along the formerly picturesque seafront, for the sake of the security of American cruiseship passengers. A taxi driver in New York,

The Ethnic Elite

In Western Europe and North America, it is customary to think of ethnic minorities in terms of discrimination and deprivation. However, in large parts of the world, ethnic minorities constitute elites. Some of the standards imposed on countries by global agencies (like the IMF) and powerful states (like the USA) have created new tensions pitting the majorities against the ethnic elites. Within a dominant mode of thought, a multi-party democratic political system is favoured, as is market liberalism. These entities, it is widely believed, will make the world a better place. This is assumed in the foreign policy of the rich countries, in trade agreements and in leading development organizations.

Against this background, the American law professor Amy Chua's book *World on Fire* (Chua 2003) deserves attention. Her argument is that the competence, networks and work ethic of ethnic elites in many countries contribute to added value to the benefit of all of society. When society is pressured to introduce multiparty democracy and ideas about equality are allowed to spread, frustrations and hatred are directed towards the 'market dominant minorities'. The outcome may be riots and ensuing economic chaos.

It is easy to find examples that seem to confirm this general description. In Chua's country of origin, the Philippines, 1 per cent of the population (the Chinese) control 60 per cent of the economy. The Tutsi in Rwanda and Burundi may also be seen as a market-dominant minority — at least that is how they were seen by the Hutu. Chua also speaks of Jews in Russia, Lebanese in West Africa, Indians in East Africa, Chinese in South-East Asia and whites in southern Africa.

originally from El Salvador, told the British writer Tariq Ali (2002) that he supported al-Qaeda because the US, in his view, had destroyed his own country and forced him to migrate. Other wars, such as Israel's attack on Lebanon in the summer of 2006, are indirectly connected to this transnational campaign.

Fifth and lastly, but not least in importance, the 'war on terror' indicates that the attention of others, and their respect, are in short supply in an era of global communication. Osama bin Laden and his ideological allies rarely speak of imperialism and global capitalism as their adversaries, but often use words like 'respect', 'dignity' and 'humiliation'. Many non-Americans have been struck by the ease with which the US 'accidentally' kills large numbers of civilians during their campaigns against a particular government or a particular terrorist group. This has led many to conclude that a Muslim life has a much lower value than an American one. Writing a few years before the 9/11 attacks, Castells (1998) prophesied that

She also has interesting views on Latin America, where a conspicuous proportion of the elites are of purely European descent.

The tensions and riots described by Chua, which doubtless create economic chaos, not to mention massive loss of life, in many countries, are connected to transnational processes in at least two ways. The conditions for the targeting of successful ethnic elites are transnational – ideas about rights and equality, and transnational business engaged in by the elites. Moreover, many ethnic elites participate modestly in domestic politics, and make moderate contributions to the domestic economy. They often invest overseas and have strong obligations towards co-ethnics elsewhere.

Chua's solution consists in delaying the introduction of democratic rights until basic welfare provisions are in place. Another alternative might be to regulate the huge income differences between the elites and the majority through progressive taxation, and to create incentives for members of the majority to engage in the businesses controlled by the ethnic elites.

Towards the end of her book, Chua notes that the US government's 'ethnic policy for Iraq was essentially to have no ethnic policy. Instead, US officials seemed strangely confident that Iraq's ethnic, religious, and tribal division would dissipate in the face of democracy and market-generated wealth' (Chua 2003: 291). She here indicates a main source of vulnerability in the contemporary world, caused by the tensions wrought by globalization.

international terrorism would be the main security threat in the rich countries in the global network society. At the time of writing, he seems to have been proven right, notwithstanding the fact that the number of people killed by terrorists remains very low compared with almost any other cause of death. As Furedi rightly points out (Furedi 2002), what we fear is rarely that which actually kills us.

Did 11 September 2001 represent a turning point in the short history of the post-Cold War world? I have speculated, at the outset of this chapter (and, at greater length, in Eriksen 2001b), that while the 1990s was an optimistic decade where globalization was generally associated (in the rich North Atlantic societies) with openness, communication, prosperity, human rights and peace, the world entered a paranoid phase of globalization with the terrorist attacks. Suddenly, the Internet was not the main metaphor for globalization; it was terrorism.

This, we may be allowed to hope, is too bleak a prospect. It should be kept in mind that globalization is not a process with a particular direction, it is not directed towards a specified end. Ideas about human rights and democracy continue to spread; the battle against some dreadful diseases is successful; migration gives new hopes to millions of people; and global communication makes global solidarity and a cosmopolitan outlook possible in ways that were unthinkable two generations ago. At the same time, globalization also entails the spread of deadly diseases, destructive ideas and practices, fundamentalism and paranoia, drugs and weapons. It brings us closer to each other through instantaneous communication and travel, but it also brings us further from each other by continuously reminding us of the deep differences in values, lifestyle and opportunity which continues to divide us, probably more painfully than ever before.

P.S. Having finished this chapter just after midnight, I fired up my web browser to read the latest news. A main item in the local newspapers tonight (in Oslo) was a story about a 'suspicious note' found by cabin personnel in a Norwegian Airlines plane between two flights. The note seemed to contain the word 'virus bomb' (*virusbombe*), and the flight was delayed because of further checks. The spokeswoman for the airline explained that 'the text was a bit ambiguous, so we chose not to take any chances'. A few hours later, it was clear that no terrorist attack was planned on the domestic flight from Oslo to Trondheim but the story says a thing or two about the relevance of this chapter's topic.

Chapter Summary

- Globalization changes the risk environment because of increased interdependence and ensuing vulnerability.
- Risk perception rarely corresponds with objective risk: what we fear rarely kills us.
- Climate change is simultaneously a result of (economic and technological) globalization and an example of a truly global risk.
- Transnational terrorism contributes to breaking down the boundaries between a society's inside and outside.
- Common policy dilemmas in the context of serious perceived risk consist in the tension between security and rights.

8 RE-EMBEDDING

Neo-tribal and fundamentalist tendencies, which reflect and articulate the experience of people on the receiving end of globalization, are as much legitimate offspring of globalization as the widely acclaimed 'hybridization' of top culture – the culture at the globalized top.

Zygmunt Bauman

INTRODUCTION

This book has shown that, in an important sense, the human world is presently more tightly integrated than at any earlier point in history. In the age of the jet plane and satellite dish, the age of global capitalism, the age of ubiquitous markets and transnational mediascapes, it is time and again claimed that the world is rapidly becoming a single place. Yet, a perhaps even more striking development of the post-Cold War world is the emergence – seemingly everywhere – of identity politics whose explicit aim is the restoration of rooted tradition, religious fervour or commitment to ethnic or national identities, majoritarian and minoritarian.

I have said, in many different ways, that globalization is always *glocal* in the sense that human lives take place in particular locations – even if they are transnational, on the move, dislocated. Anthropologists have written about the *indigenization of modernity* (Sahlins 1994), showing how modern artefacts and practices are incorporated into pre-existing worlds of meaning, modifying them somewhat, but not homogenizing them. Many of the dimensions of modernity seen as uniform worldwide, such as bureaucracies, markets, computer networks and human rights discourses, always take on a distinctly local character, not to mention consumption: A trip to McDonald's triggers an entirely different set of cultural connotations in Amsterdam from what it does in Chicago, not to mention Beijing.

Some writers on globalization have argued that the shrinking of the world will almost inevitably lead to a new value orientation, some indeed heralding the coming of a new kind of person (see, for instance, W. T. Anderson 1999). These writers, who seem to proclaim the advent of a new man, or at least new set of uprooted, deterritorialized values, are often accused of generalizing from their own North Atlantic middle-class habitus. The sociologist John Urry, lending himself easily to this criticism, argues in the final chapter of his *Global Complexity* (2003) that globalization has the potential to stimulate widespread cosmopolitanism (however, he does not say among whom). But, as Urry readily admits in an earlier chapter in the same book, the principles of closeness and distance still hold, for example in viewing patterns on television, where a global trend consists in viewers' preferences for locally produced programmes.

In other words, the disembedding characteristic of globalization creates global homogeneity only at a very superficial level. It creates a global grammar of comparison enabling communication and exchange to be channelled relatively easily across borders. It thereby stimulates an awareness of difference.

Globalization is dual and operates, one might say, through dialectical negation: It *shrinks* the world by facilitating fast contact across former boundaries, and it *expands* the world by creating an awareness of difference. It *homogenizes* human lives by imposing a set of common denominators (state organization, labour markets, consumption and so forth), but it also leads to *heterogenization* through the new forms of diversity emerging from the intensified contact. Globalization is *centripetal* in that it connects people worldwide; and it is *centrifugal* in that it inspires a heightened awareness of, and indeed (re)constructions of local uniqueness. It centralizes power and prompts movements, among indigenous peoples, small nations and others, fighting for local autonomy and self-determination. Finally, globalization makes a universalist *cosmopolitanism* possible in political thought and action because it reminds us that we are all in the same boat and have to live together in spite of our mutual differences; but it also encourages *fundamentalism* and various forms of missionary universalism as well as parochial localism, because global integration leads to a sense of alienation threatening identities and notions of political sovereignty.

Third ways or third alternatives are often created through the working out of these tensions. This is, among other things, where the term *glocalization* comes into its own.

An important insight from recent studies of modernities is the fact that modernization and increasing scale in social organization are marked by a complex process of simultaneous homogenization and differentiation. Some differences vanish, whereas others emerge. As Jonathan Friedman (1990: 311) puts it: 'Ethnic and cultural fragmentation and modernist homogenization are not two arguments, two opposing views of what is happening in the world today, but two constitutive trends of global reality.'

Phrased more generally, *disembedding* is always countered by *re-embedding*. The more abstract the power, the sources of personal identity, the media flows and the commodities available in the market become, the greater will the perceived need be to strengthen and sometimes recreate (or even invent) local foundations for political action and personal identity, locally produced books and songs, products with the smell, the sound, the taste of home. We cannot generalize bluntly about this: many people are perfectly happy to live in a disembedded world, and hundreds of millions are so poor, disenfranchised and marginalized that the problem never occurs to them – or if it does, it appears as a dream of slick affluence. Yet, re-embedding processes are sufficiently comprehensive, varied and influential to justify their place at the end of this, admittedly convoluted and selective, journey through some of the main dimensions of globalization.

While, as a student in the mid-1980s, I was planning my first fieldwork in Mauritius, recognizing the ethnic plurality of its population and the mixed composition of settlements, I imagined Mauritians to have a profoundly reflexive, negotiable and ambivalent attitude to cultural practices and ethnic identity. Being confronted with a bewildering array of options, epitomized in the everyday lives of their neighbours, I expected them to treat group identification with ironic distance. This did not turn out to be the case. In fact, the majority of Mauritians took their own notions and conventions for granted, more or less ignoring what their neighbours were up to. Moreover, the social universe inhabited by most Mauritians was much simpler than an assessment of the actual ethnic diversity of the island would lead one to expect. Categories were lumped and taxonomies were simplified, and group identification was usually taken for granted. This reminds us of the trivial, but often-forgotten fact that cosmopolitan societies do not necessarily create cosmopolitans; that globalization does not create global people. 'The social thickness of the global' spoken of by Sassen (2003: 262) refers to the webs of commitment, sometimes spanning thousands of kilometres, cultivated by denizens of transnational space (see Lien and Melhuus 2007 for cases).

In other words, millions of people are transnational in the sense that they maintain important ties of obligations across vast distances. Upon close examination of these transnational ties, it often turns out that they resemble the old ties in the sense that they build on similar commonalities and obligations.

1 IDENTITY POLITICS AS A RESPONSE TO GLOBALIZATION

Recent years have witnessed the growth, in societies in all continents, of political movements seeking to strengthen the collective sense of uniqueness, often targeting globalization processes, which are seen as a threat to local distinctiveness and self-determination. A European example with tragic consequences is the rise of ethnic nationalism in Croatia and Serbia from the 1980s, but even in the more prosperous and stable European Union, strong ethnic and nationalist movements grew during the 1990s and into the new millennium, ranging from Scottish separatism to the anti-immigration Front National in France and nationalist populism in countries like Austria, Denmark and the Netherlands. In Asia, two of the most powerful examples from recent history were the rise of the Taliban to power in Afghanistan and the meteoric success of the Hindu nationalist BJP in India; and many African countries have also seen a strong ethnification of their politics during the last decade-and-a-half, as well as the rise of political Islam in the Sahel and the north. In the Americas, various minority movements, from indigenous groups to African Americans, have with increasing success demanded cultural recognition and equal rights. In sum, politics around the turn of the millennium has to a great extent meant identity politics.

This new political scene, difficult to fit into the old left-right divide, is interpreted in very different ways by the many academics and journalists who have studied them. This is partly because identity politics comes in many flavours: some are separatist nationalist movements; some represent historically oppressed minorities which demand equal rights; some are dominant groups trying to prevent minorities from gaining access to national resources; some are religious, some are ethnic, and some are regional. At the very least, identity politics from above must be distinguished from identity politics from below.

Many writers see identity politics in general as an anti-modern counterreaction to the individualism and freedom enhanced by globalization, while others see it as the defence of the weak against foreign dominance, or even as a strategy of modernization using the language of tradition to garner popular support. Some emphasize the psychological dimension of identity politics, seeing it as nostalgic attempts to retain dignity and a sense of rootedness in an era of rapid change; others focus on competition for scarce resources between groups; some see identity politics as a strategy of exclusion and an ideology of hatred, whereas yet others see it as the trueborn child of socialism, as an expression of the collective strivings of the underdog.

None of these interpretations and judgements tells the whole story, both because the concrete movements in question differ and because the phenomenon of identity politics is too complex for a simple explanation to suffice. What is clear, however, is that the centripetal or unifying forces of globalization and the centrifugal or fragmenting forces of identity politics are two sides of the same coin, two complementary tendencies that must be understood well by anyone wishing to make sense of the global scene at the turn of the millennium.

For a variety of reasons, globalization creates the conditions for *localization*, that is various kinds of attempts at creating bounded entities – countries (nationalism or separatism), faith systems (religious revitalization), cultures (linguistic or cultural movements) or interest groups (ethnicity). For this reason, a more apt term is glocalization. Let us now move to a general description of some features that the 'glocal' identity movements of the turn of the millennium seem to have in common – the rudiments of a grammar of identity politics.

First, identity politics always entails *competition over scarce resources*. Successful mobilization on the basis of collective identities presupposes a widespread belief that resources are unequally distributed along group lines. 'Resources' should be interpreted in the widest sense possible and could in principle be taken to mean economic wealth or political power, recognition or symbolic power. What is at stake can be economic or political resources but the *recognition of others* has been an underestimated, scarce resource, as well as meaningful social attachments where one is in command of one's own life to an acceptable degree.

Secondly, *modernization and globalization actualize differences and trigger conflict.* When formerly discrete groups are integrated into shared economic and political systems, inequalities are made visible because direct comparison between the groups becomes possible. Friction occurs frequently. In a certain sense, ethnicity can be described as the process of making cultural differences comparable, and to that extent, it is a modern phenomenon boosted by the intensified contact entailed by globalization. You do not envy your neighbour if you are unaware of his existence.

Thirdly, *similarity overrules equality ideologically.* Ethnic nationalism, politicized religion and indigenous movements all depict the in-group as homogeneous, as people 'of the same kind'. Internal differences are glossed over and, for this reason, it can often be argued that identity politics serves the interests of the privileged segments of the group, even if the group as a whole is underprivileged, because it conceals internal class differences.

Fourthly, *images of past suffering and injustice are invoked.* To mention a few examples: In the 1990s, Serbs bemoaned the defeat at the hands of the Turks in Kosovo in 1389; leaders of the Hindu BJP have taken great pains to depict Mughal

(Muslim) rule in India from the 1500s as bloody and authoritarian; and the African-American movement draws extensively on the history of slavery. Even spokesmen for clearly privileged groups, such as anti-immigrant politicians in western Europe, may argue along these lines.

Fifthly, *the political symbolism and rhetoric evokes personal experiences.* This is perhaps the most important ideological feature of identity politics in general. Using myths, cultural symbols and kinship terminology in addressing their supporters, promoters of identity politics try to downplay the difference between personal experiences and group history. In this way, it became perfectly sensible for a Serb, in the 1990s, to talk about the legendary battle of Kosovo in the first person ('*we* lost in 1389'). The logic of revenge is extended to include metaphorical kin, in many cases millions of people. The intimate experiences associated with locality and family are thereby projected onto a national screen.

Sixthly, *first-comers are contrasted with invaders.* Although this ideological feature is by no means universal in identity politics, it tends to be invoked whenever possible and, in the process, historical facts are frequently stretched.

Finally, *the actual social complexity in society is reduced to a set of simple contrasts.* As Adolf Hitler already wrote in *Mein Kampf,* the truly national leader concentrates the attention of his people on one enemy at the time. Since cross-cutting ties reduce the chances of violent conflict, the collective identity must be based on relatively unambiguous criteria (such as place, religion, mother-tongue, kinship). Again, internal differences are undercommunicated in the act of delineating boundaries towards the frequently demonized Other.

Identity politics is a trueborn child of globalization. The more similar we become, the more different we try to be. Paradoxically, however, the more different we try to be, the more similar we become – since most of us try to be different in roughly the same ways worldwide.

Against the view that identity politics is somehow anachronistic, it has been argued many times, always correctly, that although it tends to be dressed in traditional garb, beneath the surface it is a product of modernity and its associated dilemmas of identity. The strong emotions associated with a tradition, a culture or a religion can never be mobilized unless people feel that it is under siege.

Viewed in this way, the collective emotions that identity politics depend on reveal themselves to be deeply *modern* emotions associated with the sense of loss experienced in situations of rapid change, disembedding and deterritorialization. The need for security, belonging and enduring social ties based on trust is universal and cannot be wished away. Ethnic nationalism, minority movements and politicized religion offer a larger share of the cake as well as a positive sense of self, and these movements are bound to remain influential in large parts of the world.

2 THE CASE OF INDIGENOUS PEOPLES

Indigenous peoples are usually defined as ethnic groups associated with a non-industrial mode of production and a stateless political organization (cf. Eriksen 2002). The identity politics engaged in by such groups differ from that of nations and migrant minorities in that territorial autonomy and cultural self-determination are their main political goals. Engulfed by dominant states and increasingly incorporated into the global economy, indigenous groups fight legal battles on many fronts, claiming rights to land and water, language, their own artistic production and political autonomy.

The forms of resistance engaged in by indigenous movements are diverse, ranging from institutional politics among the Sami of northern Scandinavia, who have separate parliaments with limited power, to the armed uprising among Maya peasants of Chiapas in southern Mexico, and less spectacular forms of everyday resistance. However, as Hall and Fenelon (2004) point out in an important review of indigeneity and globalization, indigenous struggles against globalized external dominance tend to differ from class-based struggles through their emphasis on local community, identity politics, land claims, and rights to a variety of traditional practices, which include alternative family organizations such as matrilineality and/or polygyny, communal ownership of resources such as land, the use of land for sacred ceremonies, and indigenous knowledge, that occasionally includes use of psychoactive substances (Hall and Fenelon 2004: 156).

Although indigenous groups may occasionally profit economically from global integration, their identity depends on a certain degree of political autonomy. Following Hall and Fenelon (2004), we may say that states have traditionally subdued indigenous groups through genocide (extermination), ethnocide (their enforced assimilation into the majority) or culturicide (the destruction of group culture, if not necessarily group identity). In defending their group identity as well as the cultural content of this identity, indigenous groups run into a broad range of problems, some of them to do with human rights, national law and the universal rights and obligations of citizenship; some simply to do with the brute force of the state and capitalism – indigenous peoples usually reject private property in favour of the communal ownership or stewardship of resources. A final set of problems pertain to the character and nature of 'indigenous culture', which is, like all other culture, influenced and transformed by reflexive modernity. What exactly does it mean to be a Lakota, a San and an Inuit? Such issues are discussed vividly among scholars and indigenous peoples alike, but it must still be stressed that their main struggle is over land rights with accompanying political autonomy. Paradoxically, perhaps, many indigenous peoples have been assisted in their quest for self-determination by transnational agencies and even global organizations such as the World Council of Indigenous Peoples (WCIP), levelling pressure on nation-states from a transnational or supranational point of leverage.

3 RE-EMBEDDING IN DIASPORAS

National and other modern identities founded in traditionalist ideologies (they claim, persuasively, to be pre-modern) have proved to be extremely resilient. The enthusiasm for the proposed European Constitution in the EU member states is very modest, and the Constitution has failed to get a majority in any of the countries that have held referendums. Identification with national football teams in Europe and South America remains very strong, ethnic networks giving career opportunities for members of the in-group in polyethnic societies are thriving in many parts of the world, religions demanding the undiluted loyalty of their followers are on the rise, and everywhere, most people seem to prefer to watch locally produced programmes on TV.

The human need for secure belonging in a community, however abstract (such as a nation or a religion of conversion), seems to be an anthropological constant, but it can be satisfied in many different ways and dealt with politically in different ways, too. Commitment to a group, which forms part of a larger, plural social universe, does not necessarily lead to xenophobia and conflict; it may equally well result in cosmopolitan tolerance (see Appiah 2006 on cosmopolitanism and Hannerz 1989 on 'the global ecumene').

Creating a sense of security in an environment that changes rapidly can be hard work and it seems particularly difficult for transnational migrants and their descendants, who are confronted with opposing pressures from their immediate surroundings. The states in which they live may demand their full and undivided loyalty, or they may do quite the opposite and deny them citizenship and political rights. Both alternatives create stress and ambiguity among migrants. The classic modern notion of citizenship as the sole key to political identity is difficult to maintain at a time when dual loyalties, exile and movement are widespread.

Solutions to dilemmas of identity and belonging among uprooted people vary. Some seek to be assimilated in the new country and effectively to change their group identity. This has to a great extent happened over the last 150 years with Poles in Germany and Swedes in Norway, but not with Irish in Britain. With transnational migrants who may have a different skin colour and religion from the majority, full assimilation does not seem to take place anywhere, although New World countries like the US and Canada have a more open-ended national identity than most Old

World countries, from Ireland to Japan. As a rule, migrants and their children remain attached to their country of origin. The tie tends to be weakened in the second generation, whose members have more invested in the new country than their parents, but what happens in the third generation depends to a great extent on the ability of the host country to expand its national identity to encompass the descendants of relatively recent migrants.

Whether or not full assimilation is possible, most migrants and their children retain important transnational ties (Eriksen 2007a, see R. Cohen 1997 for a wealth of historical and contemporary examples) and draw extensively on ethnic or religious networks in the new country. Far from being the fragmented and alienated people one might expect migrants to be, given their ambiguous political and cultural position, they tend, broadly, to reproduce important aspects of their original culture in the new setting. This is often met with animosity in sections of the majority population, who may insist that the newcomers do their best to 'adapt' to the host society; but at the same time, this option is often closed to immigrants who face discrimination and differential treatment from the majority. A connection to a homeland, be it the tiny Caribbean island of Nevis (Olwig 2003) or a future independent Kurdistan, gives a sense of attachment that can otherwise be difficult to develop in alien surroundings. The cultural conservatism often witnessed in migrant populations, not least among Muslims in Europe, is understandable as a reaction to hostility and indifference in the majority population. Moreover, as James Rosenau has argued in a number of works (such as Rosenau 1990), the authority of the state has become increasingly problematic not only with respect to immigrants but in general, because of increased 'turbulence' and uncertainty – what we might call effects of globalization (cf. Croucher 2004: 51–2). The sociologist Daniel Bell, writing as early as 1973, spoke prophetically of the nation-state as being too small for some tasks and too large for others; it was too small to solve the problems facing humanity and too large to give the individual a secure sense of identity (Bell 1973).

4 THE IMPORTANCE OF TRUST

A successful immigrant entrepreneur in Oslo explained on television in 2004 that the secret of his success consisted in employing only people from his own ethnic group. He knew their fathers, their cultural idioms and their norms. He could exert moral pressure on them in a way that would have been impossible with ethnic Norwegians. This kind of practice is typical of 'ethnic entrepreneurs' everywhere. As Gray (1998: 182ff.) notes, the *guanxi* ethos of reciprocity and mutual trust is a key element in the economic success of Chinese businessmen overseas, much more important than formal agreements.

It is also known that interest-free loans among relatives are common among many moral communities consisting of migrants, as is the kind of transaction typified through the *hawala* transmission of money via middlemen from refugees to kinspeople in Somalia. First-generation Tamil migrants may in some respects be poorly integrated into greater Norwegian society, but they are tightly integrated among themselves and, in important ways, in their Sri Lankan communities, through kin and caste-based loyalties with economic, political and social dimensions.

The burning question is *what* or *who* to trust. In the classic sociology of Weber, Tönnies and their supporters it was believed that trust tended to be interpersonal in the *Gemeinschaft* or traditional society, while it would be linked to abstract institutions in the *Gesellschaft* or modern society. The citizen of a modern state is expected to trust the state, whereas the tribesman supposedly trusts his relatives and co-villagers. In fact, things are less simple. The networks of the 'network society' (Castells 1996) are often interpersonal, and what keeps them going is trust. A Manhattan banker or a Danish bureaucrat depends crucially on informal networks enabling him to do his work and to feel part of a community, just as a Turkish immigrant in Germany depends on ethnic networks to satisfy his needs, of which the sense of security is one.

Informal interpersonal networks continue to exist side-by-side with the formal organization of any society, and interpersonal trust continues to be crucial. In a society with a great deal of mobility and few historically based communities, namely the US, scholars and commentators have for years been deeply engaged in a discussion on the future of 'community'. The sociologist Robert Putnam argued, in *Bowling Alone* (2000), that civil society and the webs of commitment and trust that made up American communities were eroding – in effect that the moral communities (*Gemeinschaften*) of the US were being weakened. Putnam's perspective, and not least his concept of *social capital*, has been taken on by scholars in many countries trying to investigate the extent of trust in our changing, complex societies.

Trust presupposes familiarity, and familiarity presupposes regular contact. The amount of work invested into networks just to keep them going is tremendous in the informational network society. Think of yourself as a student or scholar. Responding to e-mails, sending and receiving SMS messages, or talking on the phone to people in conversations where the main objective consists in reminding them of your existence, is likely to take up a major proportion of your precious time. The vulnerability of moral communities based on trust and reciprocity thereby made tangible, is chronic. This does not mean that they 'no longer exist' or 'no longer exist in the West', but that keeping them operative requires continuous effort when society is complex (does not consist of a single moral community) and especially so when one's personal network is partly transnational. In this sense, Giddens (1991) is right in claiming that our era is post-traditional. Tradition no longer recommends itself – it must be defended actively; similarly, communities of trust and commitment no longer perpetuate themselves through convention, but must be guarded and nurtured. Yet they remain powerful attractors – the first place to look for ordering instances in a world of teeming movement.

The vision of the individual as a hybrid, moving, unstable entity engaging in networks of variable duration, dominant in the anthropological globalization discourse, is limiting and exaggerated. Moral commitments in relationships, cultural conservatism and coercive pressures to conform remain extremely powerful everywhere. However, they no longer encompass all of society. This is why life on the New York streets is so unsafe; the reason is not that individuals are not full members of moral communities based on trust and reciprocity but that the people they are likely to encounter in dark alleys belong to other moral communities. If I may make a brief comparison to traditional societies, this situation resembles that of intertribal encounters in highland New Guinea as described by the anthropologist Marshall Sahlins (1972). Within the tribal group, generalized reciprocity is the norm; that is, sharing based on trust. Among neighbouring people, the main kind of relationship is exchange in the market place. With total strangers, however, any kind of action, including theft ('negative reciprocity'), is legitimate. Similarly, interpersonal trust and moral commitment in plural, complex societies are unlikely to encompass everybody. The single mother of Somali origin living in Amsterdam is likely to find a sense of security among other Somalis, but not in greater Dutch society. Transnational networks are interpersonal, imbued with trust and intimacy, and these qualities form the moral basis for exchange. In order to understand globalization, it is far from sufficient to look at macro processes; we must also pay attention to the webs of trust and reciprocity that create transnationalism at the micro level – and towards the situations where reciprocity fails, creating unpayable and humiliating debts of gratitude, silencing at the receiving end of unidirectional systems of exchange, exclusion from dominant circuits, and a lack of respect. When Osama bin Laden speaks about the US or Israel, he sounds almost like a disenchanted ragamuffin: as mentioned in the last chapter, there is nothing about economic domination or world imperialism in his rhetoric, but words translated as 'arrogance' and 'humiliation' recur. The implications of not being seen and respected is clearly an underestimated affliction in the contemporary world, and a main cause of such forms of re-embedding as political Islam and ethnopolitics.

Disembedding, acceleration, standardization, interconnectedness, movement, mixing: it is easy to conjure up a vision of the world as being in constant flux. I have argued against simplistic versions of this view, and even if one is fascinated by the idea of a world in continuous movement, one has to keep in mind that different social and cultural fields are moving at different speeds and at varying length.

Truly global processes affect the conditions of people living in particular localities, creating new opportunities and new forms of vulnerability. Risks are globally shared in the era of the nuclear bomb, transnational terrorism and potential ecological disasters. On the same note, the economic conditions in particular localities frequently (some would say always) depend on events taking place elsewhere in the global system. If there is an industrial boom in Taiwan, towns in the English Midlands will be affected. If oil prices rise, that means salvation for the oil-exporting Trinidadian economy and disaster for the oil-importing, neighbouring Barbadian one.

Patterns of consumption also seem to merge in certain respects; people nearly everywhere desire similar goods, from cellphones to readymade garments. Now, a precondition for this to happen is the more or less successful implementation of certain institutional dimensions of modernity, notably that of a monetary economy – if not necessarily evenly distributed wagework and literacy. The ever-increasing transnational flow of commodities, be they material or immaterial, creates a set of common cultural denominators that appear to eradicate local distinctions. The hot-dog (*halal* or not, as the case may be), the pizza and the hamburger (or, in India, the lamburger) are truly parts of world cuisine; identical pop songs are played in identical discotheques in Costa Rica and Thailand; the same Coca-Cola commercials are shown with minimal local variations at cinemas all over the world, Harry Potter volumes are ubiquitous wherever books are sold, and so on. Investment capital, military power and world literature are being disembedded from the constraints of space; they no longer belong to a particular locality. With the development of the jet plane, the satellite dish and more recently, the Internet, distance no longer seems a limiting factor for the flow of influence, investments and cultural meaning.

Yet, disembedding is never total, and it is always counteracted by re-embedding attempts. Sometimes, re-embedding does not even seem to be required – if one cares to look, the social world in which most of humanity lives remains embedded in important respects, notwithstanding decades of intensive, technology-driven globalization. The impact of globalization – or, rather, its significance for the lives we lead – is considerable but every one-sided account is ultimately false. Warning against the view of globalization as somehow 'the outcome', or the 'end product' of modernity, Mittelman (2001: 7) writes that if 'globalization is a contested and political phenomenon, then it cannot have a predetermined outcome. A political agenda of inevitability overlooks the fact that globalization was made by humans, and, if so, can be unmade or remade by humankind.' It is far-reaching and consequential but globalizing processes are always full of contradictions, which are not likely to go away soon. Some are globalizing, some are just being globalized, and many are scarcely affected by globalization.

John Gray (2005) puts it even more strongly in a critique of a book mentioned already in the preface of this book, so it seems appropriate to end with some reflections from his essay. In a review of Thomas Friedman's *The World is Flat*, polemically entitled 'The world is round', Gray compares Friedman's belief in the 'levelling of the world' with the belief in 'unfettered' global capitalism underpinning Marx and Engels' 1848 *Communist Manifesto*, and concludes that both have been proven wrong, Friedman incidentally much sooner than Marx and Engels. Gray reminds his readers, as an antidote to Friedman's optimism on behalf of the power of global capitalism to spread prosperity worldwide, that for 200 years, 'the spread of capitalism and industrialization has gone hand in hand with war and revolution'.

Gray further argues that Friedman conflates two notions of globalization:

> the belief that we are living in a period of rapid and continuous technological innovation, which has the effect of linking up events and activities throughout the world more widely and quickly than before; and the belief that this process is leading to a single worldwide economic system. The first is an empirical proposition and plainly true, the second a groundless ideological assertion. Like Marx, Friedman elides the two. (Gray 2005)

However, Gray remarks, communication technology affects the everyday lives of people less than petroleum and electricity did. And globalization does not necessarily lead to a global free market, nor does it make the world more peaceful or more liberal.

Many of the examples in this book lend support to Gray's view. One typical consequence of globalization has been the rise or rekindling of various forms of identity politics. To Gray, al-Qaeda is just as typical a product of globalization as the World Trade Organization (see Gray 2003). Transnational capitalism creates both wealth and poverty. Millions of people – indeed hundreds of millions – will never have access to the wealth because they are simply ignored and squeezed into increasingly marginal areas, like hunter-gatherers encountering armed, well organized agriculturalists in an earlier period. The suffering of slum dwellers, dispossessed peasants, unemployed men and women in cities, victims of war and of economic exploitation, and their occasionally well orchestrated rebellions or alternative projects seeking autonomy from globalized capitalism, are the trueborn children of globalization, just as the cellphone and the Internet, the proliferation of international NGOs, the cheap tropical holiday and the growth of transnational football fandom are results of globalization. The ambiguities and paradoxes of globalization are not going away.

Chapter Summary

- The disembedding forces of globalization are complemented by re-embedding projects seeking to retain or recreate a sense of continuity, security and trust.
- Even 'disembedded' institutions take on local meanings and flavours in different societies.
- Identity politics — religious, nationalist, ethnic or regional — is a typical form of resistance to globalization, especially in its economic dimension.
- Paradoxically, identity politics insisting on the primacy of the local and unique tends to draw on globalized resources such as international NGOs and computer networks.
- Indigenous and migrant identity politics tend to pursue different goals; autonomy from and recognition by greater society, respectively.
- Any belief in TINA ('There Is No Alternative') is disproved by the myriad forms of re-embedding and resistance engaged in, but also by the exclusion of millions from global networks.

QUESTIONS FOR ESSAYS AND CLASS DISCUSSION

INTRODUCTION

1. Discuss differences and similarities between contemporary globalization and the colonial world-system of the nineteenth century.
2. In what sense does the author claim that the post-Cold War world entails a new phase of globalization? Do you agree?
3. How can identity politics be said to be an outcome of globalization?
4. What is the difference between globalization and Westernization?
5. What is meant by 'glocalization'?

I DISEMBEDDING

1. In which ways does disembedding occur as deterritorialization? Give some examples and discuss the consequences.
2. Mention three main forms of deterritorialization that are integral to modernity, and indicate how they are necessary conditions for contemporary globalization.
3. In what way does the author see musical notation as connected to globalization? Do you agree?
4. How can nationalism be said to be a product of the same forces that are shaping globalization?
5. What are some of the main differences between contemporary globalization and the modernity of the nation-state?

2 ACCELERATION

1. Describe some personal, political, cultural and economic consequences of the telegraph for transnational communication in the nineteenth century.

2. Mention a few areas where acceleration has been perceptible from your parents' generation to yours, and discuss how this process relates to globalization.
3. In what ways can acceleration of communication make people more vulnerable?
4. Why are people who are excluded from accelerating processes likely to be politically powerless?
5. The author seems to argue that the acceleration of communication, and the compression of messages into tiny packets of information, is related to globalization. How? And do you agree?

3 STANDARDIZATION

1. What does standardization have to do with globalization?
2. How does standardization in production affect transnational investments?
3. Discuss some consequences of synchronization for globalization or transnational processes in general – financial, political, interpersonal.
4. In which areas is standardization actively resisted? Give examples from your own society and a country in a different continent.
5. What does Ritzer mean by grobalization and glocalization? Is the dichotomy useful or not?
6. Do you see a structural similarity between identity politics (ethnic, religious or nationalist) and resistance to standardized consumer goods (McDonald's Microsoft etc.)?

4 INTERCONNECTEDNESS

1. What is methodological nationalism? What are the alternatives?
2. What are the main objections, among the critics of globalization theory, against the view that the world is becoming ever more interconnected and integrated? Do you have any to add yourself?
3. Does the transnationalization of economic power through large corporations lead to a change in the global power relations? Are there any indications that such a change may come about soon? And which areas are lagging behind?
4. Present the main arguments in favour of and against global governance. What is your view?
5. In what ways do transnational media enhance a subjective sense of globalization? Give examples from sports, news and entertainment, and if possible, counterexamples.

6. Contrast chosen and enforced delinking from global interconnectedness. Do they have anything in common?

5 MOVEMENT

1. In which ways are transnational links involving migrants economically important?
2. How would you describe 'the global grammar' of tourism? What are its main homogenizing features?
3. What are the main differences between the tourist and the refugee, and how do the differences shed light on global power discrepancies?
4. What is long-distance nationalism, and how can it pose problems for democracy?
5. Why does movement make it difficult to establish firm, stable group identities, and what are some of the ways in which this challenge is being met?

6 MIXING

1. What are the main arguments against the view that cultural hybridity is a product of globalization? Do you agree?
2. What are the main possible outcomes of long-term encounters between culturally different groups?
3. Mention and define four concepts used to describe cultural mixing, emphasizing their mutual differences.
4. How can world music be described as a vessel of the 'banalization of difference'?
5. The author makes a sharp contrast between cultural mixing and social identification. Explain the significance of this distinction.

7 VULNERABILITY

1. A distinction is often made between natural and manufactured risks. What is the main limitation of this perspective?
2. What could be some of the social and economic consequences of climate change and how is it that cause, effects and remedies must be seen as global in character?
3. Give a few examples of 'false alarms' resulting from fear of unmanageable global processes. Why are they so common?

4. What is the role of experts in assessing risks and why do many feel that they have failed?
5. How can politicized religion be a possible result of a heightened sense of risk and vulnerability?
6. In what way did the 9/11 terrorist attacks break down the inside/outside boundary of American society and how does this relate to globalization?

8 RE-EMBEDDING

1. In which ways does the author claim that globalization is dual?
2. What are some of the typical forms of re-embedding?
3. What are some of the elements of 'a grammar of identity politics' proposed by the author?
4. What are some central differences between the re-embedding engaged in by diaspora populations and the identity politics of indigenous peoples?
5. How can interpersonal networks based on trust be said to constitute a central dimension of globalization?

ANNOTATED GUIDE FOR FURTHER READING

Appadurai, Arjun (1996) *Modernity at Large*. Minneapolis: University of Minnesota Press.
  An influential anthropologist looks at globalization, identifying themes and methods appropriate for anthropology and arguing throughout that globalization, far from being a source of homogenization, creates tension and unevenness.

Bauman, Zygmunt (1998) *Globalization - The Human Consequences*. New York: Columbia University Press.
  Written by the famous Polish-English social theorist known for his theoretical analyses of modernity and post-modernity, this book describes new forms of inequality, surveillance and risk resulting from tighter integration.

Chua, Amy (2003) *World on Fire: How Exporting Free Market Democracy Breeds Ethnic Hatred and Global Instability*. London: Heinemann.
  Strikingly written, provocative and wide-ranging study (by a law professor, but there isn't much law here!) of the tense relationship between ethnic elites (like Chinese in Indonesia, Lebanese in West Africa etc.) and majorities in democratizing societies.

Cohen, Robin (1997) *Global Diasporas*. London: Routledge.
  A global overview, with historical depth, of diasporic populations, describing diverse migration routes and adaptations to host societies.

Flannery, Tim (2006) *The Weather Makers: The History and Future Impact of Climate Change*. London: Penguin.
  Not a strictly academic book, this is nevertheless one of the best and most authoritative studies of climate change. Amply documented, revealing vulnerability and interconnectedness, as well as adding the depth of ecological time to the study of global processes.

Frank, Andre Gunder (1998) *ReORIENT: Global Eonomy in the Asian Age*. Berkeley: University of California Press.
  A critique of world system theory by one of its long-standing supporters, this book argues against Eurocentric views of globalization. It claims that Europe was at the centre of transnational processes only for a few centuries, and that the focus has now shifted (back?) to the Pacific.

Friedman, Thomas (2005) *The World Is Flat: A Brief History of the Globalized World in the Twenty-first Century.* London: Allen Lane.

Widely read and hugely influential on public opinion and among policymakers, this book presents a linear, quite technologically determinist view of globalization. Simplistic but powerful, it has many good cases and presents a clear, if debatable point of view.

Giddens, Anthony (1999) *Runaway World: How globalization is Reshaping our Lives.* London: Profile.

Six lectures published as a small book. Here, Giddens describes six central features of globalization, arguing that we are living through a period of major transition affecting virtually everyone on the planet.

Gray, John (1998) *False Dawn: The Delusions of Global Capitalism.* London: Granta.

A critical essay about the neoliberal economy, which argues that unfettered global capitalism engenders not universal progress and prosperity, but lingering inequalities and political chaos.

Hannerz, Ulf (1996) *Transnational Connections.* London: Routledge.

A selection of essays by an anthropologist who has contributed to shaping the field, concerning itself with cultural complexities, creolization and the emergence of new forms of cultural diversity.

Huntington, Samuel (1996) *The Clash of Civilizations: Remaking of the World Order.* New York: Simon & Schuster.

A controversial but hugely influential book, it argues that contemporary conflicts are not between ideologies but between 'civilizations' based on different cultural values and ways of life.

Marling, William H. (2006) *How 'American' is globalization?* Baltimore: Johns Hopkins University Press.

Very thought-provoking and entertaining book showing, through examples from popular culture, that globalization is somehow both less and more 'American' than commonly believed.

Mittelman, James (2004) Whither Globalization? The Vortex of Knowledge and Ideology. London: Routledge. Resisting reductionist approaches seeing globalization merely as a market-driven process, the book debunks popular myths about globalization and ends with a presentation of 'alterglobalization', the grassroots movements critical of neoliberalism and/or capitalism as such.

Ritzer, George (2004) *The Globalization of Nothing.* London: Sage.

Using simple, but original dichotomies, the author argues – with examples chiefly from consumption and marketing – that globalization follows two main itineraries: homogenization and monopoly capitalism, and locally anchored adaptations to the global field.

Robertson, Roland (1992) *Globalization.* London: Sage.

A collection of highly influential essays by one of the architects of current globalization theory, the book discusses conceptualizations of the global, the history of the global system, and introduces the term 'glocalization'.

Said, Edward (1978) *Orientalism.* New York: Vintage.

A foundational text in postcolonial studies, Said's book criticizes Western scholarship about 'Orientals' for being ideologically biased and creating an image of 'the Oriental' based on prejudices masquerading as scientifically informed depictions.

Sassen, Saskia (1998) *Globalization and Its Discontents.* New York: The New Press.

Not to be confused by Joseph Stiglitz' book with the same title, Sassen argues that increasing concentration of resources and power in transnational corporations and agencies reduce accountability and make efficient politics difficult, linking migration to the argument.

Tilly, Charles (1984) *Big Structures, Large Processes, Huge Comparisons.* New York: Russel Sage.

An important precursor to later work on globalization, this book challenges 'methodological nationalism' in sociology, arguing the need to look at transnational networks and, ultimately, global processes.

Wallerstein, Immanuel (2004) . *World-Systems Analysis: An Introduction.* Durham, NC: Duke University Press.

A clear, concise introduction to world-system theory, tracing the historical itinerary of the global capitalist economy from the sixteenth century to the present.

Wolf, Eric (1982) *Europe and the People without History.* Berkeley: University of California Press.

A history of the last 500 years, written from the perspective of the colonized peoples, offering an alternative and challenging view of the processes of globalization, so often seen from a Western perspective.

GENERAL BIBLIOGRAPHY

Aas, Katja Franko (2007) 'Analyzing a World in Motion: Global Flows Meet the "Criminology of the Other"', *Theoretical Criminology*, 11: 283–303.

Ali, Tariq (2002) *The Clash of Fundamentalisms: Crusades, Jihads and Modernity*, London: Verso.

Amin, Samir (1980) *Class and Nation: Historically and in the Current Crisis*, London: Heinemann.

——, Giovanni Arrighi, Andre Gunder Frank and Immanuel Wallerstein (1982) *Dynamics of the World Economy*, New York: Monthly Review Press.

Amselle, Jean-Loup (2001) *Branchements. Anthropologie de l'universalité des cultures*, Paris: Flammarion.

Anderson, Benedict (1991 [1983]) *Imagined Communities: Reflections on the Origin and Spread of Nationalism*, London: Verso.

—— (1992) *Long Distance Nationalism: World Capitalism and the Rise of Identity Politics*, Amsterdam: CASA.

—— (2005) *Under Three Flags: Anarchism and the Post-Colonial Imagination*, London: Verso.

Anderson, Walter Truett (1999) *The Future of the Self: Inventing the Postmodern Person*, London: Jeremy Tarcher.

Appadurai, Arjun (1990) 'Being in the World: Globalization and Localization', in Mike Featherstone (ed.), *Global Culture*, London: Sage.

—— (1996) *Modernity at Large*. Minneapolis: University of Minnesota Press.

Appiah, Kwame Anthony (2003) 'Citizens of the World', in Matthew J. Gibney (ed.), *Globalizing Rights*, Oxford: Oxford University Press.

—— (2006) *Cosmopolitanism: Ethics in a World of Strangers*, London: Allen Lane.

Augé, Marc (1992) *Non-lieux: Introduction à une anthropologie de la surmodernité*, Paris: Seuil.

Barber, Benjamin (1995) *Jihad versus McWorld: How Globalism and Tribalism are Reshaping the World*, New York: Ballantine.

Barloewen, Constantin von (2003) *Anthropologie de la mondialisation*, Paris: Syrtes.

Bauman, Zygmunt (1998) *Globalization – The Human Consequences*, New York: Columbia University Press.

—— (2000) *Liquid Modernity*, Cambridge: Polity.

Bayart, Jean-François (2003) 'The Paradoxical Invention of Economic Modernity', in Arjun Appadurai (ed.), *Globalization*, Durham, NC: Duke University Press.

Beck, Ulrich (1992 [1986]) *Risk Society: Towards a New Modernity*, London: Sage.

—— (1999) *World Risk Society*, Cambridge: Polity.

—— (2000) *What is Globalization?* trans. Patrick Camiller, Cambridge: Polity.

Bell, Daniel (1973) *The Coming of Post-industrial Society: A Venture in Social Forecasting*, New York: Basic Books.

Bergson, Henri (2001 [1889]) *Sur les données immédiates de la conscience*, Paris: PUF.

Beyer, Peter (2006) *Religions in Global Society*, London: Routledge.

Bourdieu, Pierre (1996) *Sur la télévision*, Paris: Raisons d'agir.

Caplan, Pat (ed.) (2000) *Risk Revisited*, London: Pluto.

Carrier, James G. (ed.) (1997) *Meanings of the Market*, Oxford: Berg.

Castells, Manuel (1996) *The Rise of the Network Society*, Oxford: Blackwell.

—— (1998) *End of Millennium*, Oxford: Blackwell.

Castles, Stephen and Alasdair Davidson (2000) *Citizenship and Migration: Globalization and the Politics of Belonging*, London: Palgrave Macmillan.

Chase-Dunn, Christopher and Thomas Hall (1997) *Rise and Demise: Comparing World-systems*, Boulder: Westview.

Chua, Amy (2003) *World on Fire: How Exporting Free Market Democracy Breeds Ethnic Hatred and Global Instability*, London: Heinemann.

Cohen, Daniel (2006) *Globalization and its Enemies*, Boston: MIT Press.

Cohen, Robin (1997) *Global Diasporas*, London: Routledge.

Congress of the United States (2005) *Remittances: International Payments by Migrants*, Washington, DC: CBO.

Cowan, J., Dembour, M.B. and Wilson, R.A. (eds) (2001) *Culture and Rights: Anthropological Perspectives*, Cambridge: Cambridge University Press.

Croucher, Sheila (2004) *Globalization and Belonging: The Politics of Identity in a Changing World*, Lanham, MD: Rowman & Littlefield.

Crystal, David (2000) *Language Death*, Cambridge: Cambridge University Press.

Dahl, Robert A. (2000) 'Can International Organizations be Democratic: A Skeptic's View', in D. Held and A. McGrew (eds) *The Global Transformations Reader*, Cambridge: Polity.

David, P.A. (1992) 'Heros, Herds and Hysteresis in Technological History: "The Battle of the Systems" Reconsidered', *Industrial and Corporate Change*, 1: 129–80.

Davis, Mike (2006) *Planet of Slums*, London: Verso.

Diamond, Jared (1998) *Guns, Germs and Steel: A Short History of Everybody for the last 13,000 Years*, London: Random House.

Drummond, Lee (1980) 'The Cultural Continuum: A Theory of Intersystems', *Man*, 15(2): 352–74.

Eriksen, Thomas Hylland (1998) *Common Denominators: Ethnicity, Nation-Building and Compromise in Mauritius*, Oxford: Berg.

—— (2001a) *Tyrannny of the Moment: Fast and Slow Time in the Information Age*, London: Pluto.

—— (2001b) *Bak fiendebildet: Politisk islam og verden etter 11. september (Behind the Enemy Image: Political Islam and the World after 11 September)*, Oslo: Cappelen.

—— (2001c) 'Between Universalism and Relativism: A Critique of the UNESCO Concept of Culture', in J. Cowan, M.B. Dembour and R.A. Wilson (eds) *Culture and Rights: Anthropological Perspectives*, Cambridge: Cambridge University Press.

—— (2002) *Ethnicity and Nationalism: Anthropological Perspectives*, 2nd edn, London: Pluto.

—— (ed.) (2003) *Globalisation — Studies in Anthropology*, London: Pluto.

—— (2004) 'Traditionalism and Neoliberalism: The Norwegian Folk Dress in the 21st Century', in E. Kasten (ed.), *Properties of Culture – Culture as Property*, Berlin: Dietrich Reimer Verlag.

—— (2005) Risking Security. Inaugural lecture, Vrije Universiteit Amsterdam, 15 March 2005.

—— (2007a) 'Trust and Reciprocity in Transnational Flows', in M.E. Lien and M. Melhuus (eds), *Holding Worlds Together: Ethnographies of Knowing and Belonging*, Oxford: Berghahn.

—— (2007b) 'Creolisation in Anthropological Theory and in Mauritius', in Charles Stewart (ed.), *Creolization: History, Ethnography, Theory*, Walnut Creek, CA: Left Coast Press.

Fabian, Johannes (1983) *Time and the Other: How Anthropology Makes Its Object*, New York: Columbia University Press.

Fanon, Frantz (1986 [1952]) *Black Skin, White Masks*, London: Pluto.

Featherstone, Mike (ed.) (1990) *Global Culture*, London: Sage.

Feld, Steven (2003) 'A Sweet Lullaby for World Music', in Arjun Appadurai (ed.), *Globalization*, Durham, NC: Duke University Press.

Fernandez-Armesto, Felipe (1995) *Millennium: A History of The Last Thousand Years*, New York: Prentice-Hall.

—— (2000) *Civilizations*. London: Macmillan.

Flannery, Tim (2006) *The Weather Makers: The History and Future Impact of Climate Change*, London: Penguin.

Fox, Jonathan (1999) 'Clash of Civilizations or Clash of Religions: Which is a More Important Determinant of Ethnic Conflict?' *Ethnicities*, 1(3): 295–366.

Frank, Andre Gunder (1975) *On Capitalist Underdevelopment*, Oxford: Oxford University Press.

—— (1998) *ReORIENT: Global Economy in the Asian Age*, Berkeley: University of California Press.

Franklin, Adrian (2004) 'Tourism as an Ordering: Towards a New Ontology of Tourism', *Tourist Studies*, 4: 277–301.

Friedland, Roger and Deirdre Boden (eds.) (1994) *NowHere: Space, Time and Modernity*, Berkeley: University of California Press.

Friedman, Jonathan (1990) 'Being in the World: Globalization and Localization', in Mike Featherstone (ed.), *Global Culture*, London: Sage.

—— (1992) 'General Historical and Culturally Specific Properties of Global Systems', *Review*, 15(3): 335–72.

—— (1994) *Global Identity and Cultural Process*, London: Sage.

—— (2004) 'Globalization, Transnationalization and Migration: Ideologies and Realities of Global Transformation', in J. Friedman and S. Randeria (eds), *Worlds on the Move: Globalization, Migration and Cultural Security*, London: I.B. Tauris.

Friedman, Thomas (1999) *The Lexus and the Olive Tree*, New York: Farrar, Straus & Giroux.

—— *The World Is Flat: A Brief History of the Globalized World in the 21st Century*, London: Allen Lane.

Fuglerud, Øivind (1999) *Life on the Outside*, London: Pluto.

Furedi, Frank (2002) *Culture of Fear*, 2nd edn, London: Continuum.

Galtung, Johan (1999) *Johan uten land (John of No Country)*, Oslo: Aschehoug.

Gellner, Ernest (1983) *Nations and Nationalism*, Oxford: Blackwell.

Giddens, Anthony (1985) *The Nation-State and Violence*, Cambridge: Polity.

—— (1990) *The consequences of modernity*, Cambridge: Polity.

—— (1991) *Modernity and Self-Identity*, Cambridge: Polity.

—— (1999) *Runaway World: How Globalization is Reshaping our Lives*, London: Profile.

Gilpin, Robert (2002) *The Challenge of Global Capitalism: The World Economy in the 21st Century*, Princeton, NJ: Princeton University Press.

Gilroy, Paul (1993) *The Black Atlantic*, London: Verso.

Giulianotti, Richard and Roland Robertson (2004) 'The Globalization of Football: A Study in the Glocalization of the "Serious Life"', *British Journal of Sociology*, 55(4): 545–68.

Goody, Jack (1986) *The Logic of Writing and the Organization of Society*, Cambridge: Cambridge University Press.

Gray, John (1998) *False Dawn: The Delusions of Global Capitalism*, London: Granta.

—— (2003) *Al-Qaeda and What It Means to be Modern*. London: Faber.

—— (2005) 'The World is Round', *New York Review of Books*, 18 December.

Hall, Thomas D. and James V. Fenelon (2004) 'The Futures of Indigenous Peoples: 9–11 and the Trajectory of Indigenous Survival and Resistance', *Journal of World-Systems Research*, 10(1):153–97.

Halliday, Fred (2000) 'Global Governance: Prospects and Problems', in D. Held and A. McGrew (eds), *The Global Transformations Reader*, Cambridge: Polity.

Hammar, Tomas, Grete Brochmann, Kristof Tamas and Thomas Faist (eds) (1997) *International Migration, Immobility and Development: Multidisciplinary Perspectives*, Oxford: Berg.

Hannerz, Ulf (1987) 'The World in Creolization', *Africa*, 57: 546–59.

—— (1989) 'Notes on the Global Ecumene', *Public Culture*, 1: 66–75.

—— (1990) 'Cosmopolitans and Locals in World Culture', in Mike Featherstone (ed.), *Global Culture*, London: Sage.

—— (1992) *Cultural Complexity: The Social Organization of Meaning*, New York: Columbia University Press.

—— (1996) *Transnational Connections*, London: Routledge.

Hardt, Michael and Antonio Negri (2000) *Empire*, Cambridge, MA: Harvard University Press.

—— (2004) *Multitude: War and Democracy in the Age of Empires,* London: Hamish Hamilton.

Hart, Keith (1973) 'Informal Income Opportunities and Urban Employment in Ghana', *Journal of Modern African Studies,* 11: 61–89.

Harris, Nigel (2002) *Thinking the Unthinkable: The Immigrant Myth Exposed,* London: I.B. Tauris.

Harris, Olivia (1995) 'Knowing the Past: The Antinomies of Loss in Highland Bolivia', in R. Fardon (ed.), *Counterworks: Managing Diverse Knowledges,* London: Routledge.

Harvey, David (1989) *The Condition of Postmodernity: An Inquiry into the Origins of Social Change,* Oxford: Blackwell.

Held, David, Anthony Barnett and Caspar Henderson (eds) (2005) *Debating Globalization,* Cambridge: Polity/Open Democracy.

Held, David and Anthony McGrew (2000) 'The Great Globalization Debate: An Introduction', in D. Held and A. McGrew (eds), *The Global Transformations Reader,* Cambridge: Polity.

Held, David, Anthony G. McGrew, David Goldblatt, and Jonathan Perraton (1999) *Global Transformations,* Cambridge: Polity.

Hirst, Paul and Grahame Thompson (1999) *Globalization in Question,* 2nd edn, Cambridge: Polity.

Hemer, Oscar and Thomas Tufte (eds) (2005) *Media and Glocal Change: Rethinking Communication for Development,* Buenos Aires: CLACSO.

Honoré, Carl (2005) *In Praise of Slow: How a Worldwide Movement is Challenging the Cult of Speed,* London: Orion.

Horst, Heather A. (2006) 'The Blessings and Burdens of Communication: Cell Phones in Jamaican Transnational Social Fields', *Global Networks* **6**: 143–59.

Huntington, Samuel (1996) *The Clash of Civilizations: Remaking of the World Order,* New York: Simon & Schuster.

Huyssen, Andreas (2003) 'Present Pasts: Media, Politics, Amnesia', in Arjun Appadurai (ed.) *Globalization,* Durham, NC: Duke University Press.

Kant, Immanuel (2001 [1795]) 'To Eternal Peace', in I. Kant, *Basic Writings of Kant,* New York: Modern Library.

Kasten, Erich, ed. (2004) *Properties of Culture – Culture as Property,* Berlin: Dietrich Reimer Verlag.

Kearney, Michael (1995) 'The Local and the Global: The Anthropology of Globalization and Transnationalism', *Annual Review of Anthropology,* 24: 547–65.

Keys, David (1999) *Catastrophe: An Investigation into the Origins of the Modern World,* London: Century.

Klein, Naomi (1998) *No Logo: No Space, No Choice, No Jobs,* London: Picador.

Lash, Scott and John Urry (1993) *Economies of Signs and Space,* London: Sage.

Leitch, Alison (2003) 'Slow Food and the Politics of Pork Fat: Italian Food and European Identity', *Ethnos,* 68(4): 437–62.

Lévi-Strauss, Claude (1989 [1955]) *Tristes Tropiques,* London: Picador.

Lewellen, Ted C. (2002) *The Anthropology of Globalization*. Westport, CT: Bergin & Garvey.

Lien, Marianne E. (2007) 'Weeding Tasmanian Bush; Biomigration and landscape imagery', in M. E. Lien and M. Melhuus (eds) *Holding Worlds Together: Ethnographies of Knowing and Belonging*, Oxford: Berghahn.

—— and Marit Melhuus (eds) (2007) *Holding Worlds Together: Ethnographies of Knowing and Belonging*, Oxford: Berghahn.

Löfgren, Orvar (1999) *On Holiday: A History of Vacationing*, Berkeley: University of California Press.

Lovelock, James (2006) *The Revenge of Gaia: Why the Earth Is Fighting Back – And How We Can Still Save Humanity*, London: Allen Lane.

Malinowski, Bronislaw (1984 [1922]) *Argonauts of the Western Pacific*, Prospect Heights, IL: Waveland.

Margolis, Stephen E. and S. J. Liebowitz (n.d.) Path Dependence. Downloaded 16 Sept 2006 from http://wwwpub.utdallas.edu/~liebowit/palgrave/palpd.html.

Marling, William H. (2006) *How 'American' is Globalization?* Baltimore: Johns Hopkins University Press.

Martin, Bill (1998) *Listening to the Future: The Time of Progressive Rock 1968–1978*. Chicago: Open Court.

Martin, Hans-Peter and Harald Schumann (1996) *Die Globalisierungsfälle: Der Angriff auf Demokratie*. Frankfurt: Rowohlt.

McGovern, Patrick (2002) 'Globalization or Internationalization? Foreign Footballers in the English League, 1946–95', *Sociology*, 36(1): 23–42.

McLuhan, Marshall (1994 [1964]) *Understanding Media: The Extensions of Man*, London: Routledge.

McNeill, William (1976) *Plagues and Peoples*, New York: Anchor.

Meyer, John W., David H. Kamens, Aaron Benavot, Yua-Kyung Cha and Suk-Ying Wong (1992) *School Knowledge for the Masses: World Models and National Primary Curricular Categories in the Twentieth Century*, London: Falmer.

Miller, Daniel (2001) *The Dialectics of Shopping*, Chicago: University of Chicago Press.

—— and Don Slater (2000) *The Internet: An Ethnographic Approach*, Oxford: Berg.

Mittelman, James (2000) *The Globalization Syndrome*, Princeton, NJ: Princeton University Press.

—— (2001) 'Globalization: Captors and Captives', in J.H. Mittelman and N. Othman (eds) *Capturing Globalization*, London: Routledge.

Monbiot, George (2003) *The Age of Consent: A Manifesto for a New World Order*, London: Flamingo.

Morley, David (2000) *Home Territories: Media, Mobility and Identity*, London: Routledge.

—— and Kevin Robins (eds) (1995) *Spaces of Identity: Global Media, Electronic Landscapes and Cultural Boundaries*, London: Routledge.

Naipaul, V.S. (1961) *A House for Mr Biswas*, London: Andre Deutsch.

—— (1981) *Among the Believers*, London: Andre Deutsch.

—— (1987) *The Enigma of Arrival*, London: Viking.

—— (1998) *Beyond Belief: Islamic Excursions Among the Converted People*, New York: Vintage.

Ngugi wa Thiong'o (1986) *Decolonising the Mind*, London: Heinemann.

Olwig, Karen Fog (2003) 'Global Place and Place-Identities: Lessons from Caribbean Research', in T. H. Eriksen (ed.) *Globalisation – Studies in Anthropology*, London: Pluto.

Papastergiadis, Nikos (2000) *The Turbulence of Migration*, Cambridge: Cambridge University Press.

Putnam, Robert (2000) *Bowling Alone: The Collapse and Revival of American Community*, New York: Simon & Schuster.

Riccio, Bruno (1999) Senegalese Transmigrants and the Construction of Immigration in Emilia-Romagna, Italy. DPhil. thesis, University of Sussex.

Ritzer, George (1993) *The McDonaldization of Society: An Investigation into the Changing Character of Contemporary Social Life*, Newbury Park: Pine Forge Press.

—— (2004) *The Globalization of Nothing*, London: Sage.

Robertson, Roland (1992) *Globalization: Social Theory and Global Culture*, London: Sage.

Rodgers, Dennis (2004) '"Disembedding" the city: Crime, insecurity and spatial organization in Managua, Nicaragua', *Environment and Urbanization*, 16(2): 113–23.

Rosenau, James (1990) *Turbulence in World Politics: A Theory of Change and Continuity*, Princeton, NJ: Princeton University Press.

Rostow, Walt (1960) *The Stages of Economic Growth: A Non-Communist Manifesto*, Cambridge: Cambridge University Press.

Rushdie, Salman (1988) *The Satanic Verses*, London: Viking.

—— (1991) *Imaginary Homelands*, London: Granta.

—— (2001) *Fury*, New York: Random House.

Sahlins, Marshall D. (1972) *Stone Age Economics*, Chicago: Aldine.

—— (1994) 'Goodbye to Tristes Tropes: Ethnography in the Context of Modern World History', in Robert Borofsky (ed.), *Assessing Cultural Anthropology*, New York: McGraw-Hill.

Said, Edward (1978) *Orientalism*, New York: Vintage.

Sassen, Saskia (1998) *Globalization and its Discontents*, New York: The New Press.

—— (2003) 'Spatialities and Temporalities of the Global: Elements for a Theorization', in Arjun Appadurai (ed.), *Globalization*, Durham, NC: Duke University Press.

—— (2006) *Territory, Authority, Rights: From Medieval to Global Assemblages*, Princeton, N.J.: Princeton University Press.

Schiller, Nina Glick, Linda Basch and Cristina Blanc-Szanton (eds) (1992) *Towards a Transnational Perspective on Migration: Race, Class, Ethnicity, and Nationalism Reconsidered*, New York: New York Academy of Sciences.

Schirato, Tony and Jen Webb (2003) *Understanding Globalization*, London: Sage.

Scholte, Jan Aart (2005) *Globalization: A Critical Introduction*, 2nd edn. London: Palgrave.

Sennett, Richard (1997) *The Corrosion of Character: The Personal Consequences of Work in the New Capitalism*, New York: W.W. Norton.

Sinding-Larsen, Henrik (1991) 'Computers, Musical Notation and the Externalisation of Knowledge: Towards a Comparative Study in the History of Information Technology', in Massimo Negrotti (ed.), *Understanding the Artificial: On the Future Shape of Artificial Intelligence*, London: Springer-Verlag.

Sklair, Leslie (2002) *Globalization: Capitalism and Its Alternatives*, 3rd edn, Oxford: Oxford University Press.

Smith, A.D. (1991) *National Identity*, London: Penguin.

Soros, George (2002) *George Soros on Globalization*, Oxford: Public Affairs.

Stewart, Charles (ed.) (2007) *Creolization: History, Ethnography, Theory*, Walnut Creek, CA: Left Coast Press.

Stiglitz, Joseph (2002) *Globalization and its Discontents*, London: Allen Lane.

Strathern, Marilyn (ed.) (1995) *Shifting Contexts: Transformations in Anthropological Knowledge*, London: Routledge.

Steger, Manfred (2003) *Globalization: A Very Short Introduction*, Oxford: Oxford University Press.

Tambs-Lyche, Harald (1980) *London Patidars*, London: Routledge.

Thrift, Nigel (1999) 'The Place of Complexity', *Theory, Culture and Society*, 16: 31–70.

Tilly, Charles (1984) *Big Structures, Large Processes, Huge Comparisons*, New York: Russel Sage.

Traufetter, G. (2006) 'Ackerbau auf Grönland' (Agriculture in Greenland), *Der Spiegel*, 28 August.

UNESCO (1995) *Our Creative Diversity*, Paris: UNESCO.

Urry, John (1990) *The Tourist Gaze: Leisure and Travel in Contemporary Societies*, London: Sage.

—— (2000) *Sociology Beyond Societies*, Cambridge: Polity.

—— (2003) *Global Complexity*, Cambridge: Polity.

Vertovec, Steven (2004) Cheap Calls: The Social Clue of Migrant Transnationalism, *Global Networks*, 4: 219–24.

—— (2006) *The Emergence of Super-Diversity in Britain*, Oxford: COMPAS, Working Paper WP-06-25.

Virilio, Paul (1996) *Cybermonde: le politique du pire*, Paris: Philippe Petit.

—— (2000) *The Information Bomb*, London: Verso.

Wallerstein, Immanuel (1974–79) *The Modern World-System* (3 vols), New York: Academic Press.

—— (2004) *World-Systems Analysis: An Introduction*. Durham, NC: Duke University Press.

Waters, Malcolm (2001) *Globalization*, 2nd edn, London: Routledge.

Wilson, Richard A. (ed.) (1997) *Human Rights, Culture and Context*, London: Pluto.

—— (2005) *Human Rights in the 'War on Terror'*. Cambridge: Cambridge University Press.

Wisner, Ben, Piers Blaikie, Terry Cannon and Ian Davis (2004) *At Risk: Natural Hazards, People's Vulnerability and Disasters*, revised edn, London: Routledge.

Wolf, Eric (1982) *Europe and the People without History*, Berkeley: University of California Press.

Worsley, Peter (1984) *The Three Worlds. Culture and World Development*, London: Weidenfeld & Nicolson.

INDEX